A Month of Sundays

by

Glenda Jones

Glenda Jones
4041 Carroll Side Road,
R.R. 2, Carp,
Ontario, Canada K0A 1L0

Telephone: (613) 256-6479
Email: monthofsundays.glenda@gmail.com

Cover illustration: A watercolour painting by the author, Glenda Jones.

Library and Archives Canada Cataloguing in Publication

Jones, Glenda, 1942-
      A month of Sundays / by Glenda Jones.

Short stories originally published in The Humm.
ISBN 978-0-9784492-0-9

        1. Jones, Glenda, 1942- --Anecdotes. 2. Almonte (Ont.)--Anecdotes.
I. Title. II. Title: Humm (Almonte, Ont.).

PS8375.J65 2007   C818'.603   C2007-905363-7

Printed in Canada
1st Edition 2007

To the memory of my Mom,
who gave me her best sayings.

INTRODUCTION

It could have been the alignment of the stars in the millennium year; it could have been fate. I choose to think it was pure serendipity. Now, there's a thought to contemplate. Life rolls along with chance encounters we might otherwise ignore, except that they occasionally interlock with surprising results.

In 2000 I tentatively offered up one essay to *The Humm*, hoping that it would be worthy of print. It was, and now seven years later these monthly musings that are a regular feature of the paper have provided enough material for a whole book. Oh, it took some nagging from *Humm* readers before I was ready to seize the day, and go for it. But again serendipity stepped in when I met a neighbour in the publishing business.

This collection has much to do with my take on daily occurrences, nothing earth-shaking, but rather conclusions at which I have arrived by observance. Some have delighted me; some have angered me. All have given me an excuse to write, and for that I am thankful. I don't have to look far for inspiration, what with my dear family and my community close at hand. They are my life and as such have a starring role in these essays.

A word from the "wiser-now": people cannot say they "live" in a community unless they are willing to pitch in their talents and time. You know the old maxims: you reap what you sow; actions speak louder than words, etc. Well, they are true, and the only way to enjoy the full measure of your life is to share it with others. This is especially true in a small town like Almonte, ON. As relative newcomers, having been here only twelve years, we hope we are now seen as belonging. We have friends and connections here that we love. It's where we want to stay forever.

Never in a month of Sundays did I imagine that the *Reever Report* would strike such a sympathetic chord with *The Humm* readers. We all enjoy life's peculiar little connections and, on reflection, I am ever so grateful that the day I offered up that first tentative essay, Kris Riendeau, *The Humm* editor, agreed to run it.

My thanks go to Kris and Rob Riendeau for their continued support. Also, thanks to the many readers, in particular Anne Wheatley, who gave me the book idea in the first place. Her encouragement has been heart-warming.

However, none of this would have been possible without Alan. We embarked on this marvelous adventure together, and every day has brought us something new and exciting. Our family not only has supplied me with much material, but also has been very supportive in my efforts. I hope seeing their lives in print will not be traumatic!

So make a cup of tea, and turn the page.

TABLE OF CONTENTS

Continued

Table of Contents Continued

"You just never know; that's what makes life so exciting." Our daughter, Alison gave us this maxim shortly before we moved to the country and, oh boy, it has come in handy to explain some of the encounters we've had out here. We were city folks, but thanks to our generous neighbours, we have been able to embrace our rural surrounding with only a few stumbles along the way.

CATTLE ROUND-UP ON CARROLL SIDE ROAD

We're not really isolated out here on Carroll Side Road; we have neighbours on either side, but not so close we're on each other's doorsteps, and we all have acreage on which to play. We have wild life, to be sure. Deer, the occasional fox, a chicken-devouring fisher, and a black bear and cubs have all made appearances over the years. It keeps us on our toes, and reminds us that even though we think we own this land, it really belongs to nature.

In general, however, we are pretty domesticated. Our side road features a marvelous assortment of dogs, our little Sheltie, our neighbour's black Lab, a huge retriever, a gracefully-ageing golden Lab, a collie, and a whirling dervish Australian cattle dog affectionately called Yippie. A few chickens, a few ducks, some obstreperous geese, and a herd of cows create their own symphony as we walk the road. Country living doesn't get any better!

Now, usually these animals are well under control, but occasionally things go awry. One day as we drove blithely over the rise of our hill, we came to a screeching stop, confronted with the docile stare of three large calves standing in the middle of the road. First they looked startled, not unlike school kids caught playing hooky. But in fact that stare was defiance, and we could tell we were not proceeding farther. We slowly backed up the road; they stood their ground. We were stumped as to our next move, and thought it best to call their owner. Well, sir, the farmer was out his door and up the hill in his pickup in a flash! He commandeered Alan to hop in and drive, while he tried to herd his cows back behind the fence line.

"Don't let them head for the highway," he shouted, while he whistled and stomped to attract bovine attention. Alan was in his glory: driving a real farm truck, (That's manual transmission there!) following real cattle! I thought I heard him yell "Yippie kay-ay", but I might have been mistaken. I was playing it cool, the casual observer, until all of a sudden the cows turned tail and started my direction. When those calves came trotting down the hill towards me and the eventual highway if they didn't veer left, they looked mighty big. There came the farmer, charging after them waving his arms and shouting, and at the last possible moment as I felt all the blood rush from my veins, the whole shebang roared past and over the fence line. The last I looked they were snorting and pawing the ground as the poor farmer wiped his forehead and called an epithet or two after their twitching tails. I was mighty glad to see them safely in the field, bawling their heads off as if we had thwarted their afternoon of freedom.

The farmer hauled out the tools and repaired the fence before our newest neighbours returned from their holidays. Susie and Terri are transplanted Americans revelling in the Canadian country life. The wildlife in particular fascinates them. They've got photos of all the wild visitors, have decorated their home like a hunting lodge, and couldn't be more Canadian if they had the big red and white flag in their front yard.

They arrived home late at night, totally unaware of the previous escapade. The next morning, Susie went out to find huge tracks all over her yard. She measured them, and called to tell us how some huge animal had sampled all her bird feeders, eaten the tops of several plants, and tromped through the flower beds. She contacted the Wildlife Service to see when moose were last spotted here, and was told that, although rare, it was entirely possible. We were all duly impressed with the size of those tracks, and didn't blame Susie for passing the news along to family and friends back home. However, the head truck driver of the cattle round-up looked at those moose tracks carefully, followed them over to the mended fence, and regretfully announced that he figured the moose was now reclining passively in the lower field, a much subdued young heifer. Poor Susie was devastated.

Out here on Carroll Side Road, you just never know what will be wandering through the yard. At any moment some wild thing might be right on your back porch - like the bear cub next door. You can bet if it happens here, we'll phone everyone we know!

We all need a dog to get us outside and in touch with the elements. Our furry little Shelties practically live by the door, and we have taken to disguising the notion of a walk till we are ready to head out, or we are besieged with ecstatic barking. Their idea of the best time for a walk is every minute of the day, the more frequent the better!

VERSACE, EAT YOUR HEART OUT!

January brings a spate of fashion shows in Paris, giving us the low down on what we're going to be needing come spring. Well, that's a long way off, and in the meantime, we're creating our own fashion statement right here. And we're doing a mighty fine job too.

We all had the best intentions in November: new jacket, or at least the old one refurbished, matching hat, decent boots, and a good scarf. And didn't we look nice for the first couple of weeks? We launched into winter with the silly notion to come out the other end with some modicum of fashion sense intact.

Then came January!

Somewhere along the line, the resolve broke down, and I for one am again the epitome of utilitarianism instead of the fashion plate I aspire to be. I lost one of my brand new mitts, so now am back to the old green ones that don't match anything, but keep my hands warm. The hat was fine, but didn't keep my head warm, so I resurrected the toque that makes me look like a pinhead, and itches, but covers my ears. The dressy boots just couldn't cut it on the ice, so I had to give up on those or console myself with doing the "mince walk" all winter. However, I'm the proud owner of really substantial Ice-Walkers, the kind that strap on the big Kodiak boots so I can stride out with confidence. Just tromp around in a pair of those dandies, and watch people clear your path!

Since Belle insists on a walk at least twice a day, I'm ready! Got the boots, the hat, the old mended mitts, a scarf that is thick and long enough to cover my face, and an ever-so-elegant hood that snaps up under my chin. Add snow pants for the really cold days, and I'm a picture of fashion to behold. Now, don't you be snickering there; you know full well we all look the same.

One trip to the Big City only drives home the total lack of high fashion we have adopted to enjoy the cold. I was about half way around the mall when I caught sight of myself in a mirror. Oh my, what a beauty: snow pants, the big boots (minus the walkers), jacket a little the worse for wear, and those green mitts. Was it any wonder the clerks were ignoring me in the fashion shops? I might as well have had "country" stamped in bold letters on my forehead. And there was no way I could even ditch the jacket, since the ratty sweat-shirt under it was no picture either. Really, where had this woman come from! But was I ashamed of myself? Not a chance. It's what I need for winter, and I wouldn't dream of trading it for the Holt-Renfrew model.

Years ago when we were involved in speedskating and spending every day outdoors, I owned a bright yellow snow suit. It was great; everyone knew who I was by that suit. It was possibly the closest thing you'd find to a Big Bird costume, but it worked for me: warm, distinctive, and what the heck, just a little crazy. We do seem to identify each other in winter by our outer gear. Claire has the purple coat, Monique has the green jacket, Lorna has the blue parka, and heaven help any of us if we get a new one. No one would recognize us for a while. When I got a black suit to replace the yellow one, I became anonymous very quickly! We met one of our winter acquaintances one summer, and he nearly passed by us. "Oh," says he, "I didn't recognize you with your clothes off." That one's a classic!

The little kids amaze me. All decked out in snow pants bought a size too big so they'll last two winters (as if!), with their little hats pulled clean over their eyebrows, these little people tumble around in the snow like coloured marshmallows on angel food cake. Judging by the number of little mitts lost through a winter, I guess the old-fashioned "idiot strings" aren't tied on mitts anymore. I should have had a string on those new mitts of mine, and I'd not be resigned to the old green things now!

The only people who seem to retain their fashion sense all winter are the teen-agers, and I don't know how they do it. On the coldest days, you can catch guys running from the school to their cars in T-shirts. The girls still sport the tight low jeans and little tops under short little jackets worn open at the neck with either no scarf or a long dangling number. Mitts and boots are absolutely NOT in the picture! Well, I guess we were all young enough once to remember what keeps them warm. 'Nuff said there! I admire their stamina.

It won't be long before we can shed the outer layers. What will we do with the time we spent hauling all these winter duds on and off? What will we do with the extra space in the boot closet? And most important of all, where will we hide the extra pounds these bulky clothes have so kindly concealed over the winter? On further consideration, I think I'll take the good thick jacket over the Versace summer skirt any day!

The editors of The Humm are socially conscious people who are sensitive to many important humanitarian issues in our community. Once a year they challenge their writers to contribute to the general theme for that month. However, in February deep thought can be heavy going, not only for the writer but also for the reader.

WHAT IS LEFT OF HUMAN RIGHTS?

There is little doubt that supporters for human rights have made major contributions to society. We take them for granted, not questioning how they work, but knowing they get the job done, so to speak. While most people will advocate strongly for human rights, the topic does raise issues for some. In fact, those of us who would not advocate for human rights would be considered out of step, on the wrong side, and quite frankly, even gauche!

(Are you scandalized yet?) Well, wait. I know there are a lot of us out here who would agree with me, including many of our leaders, artists, and politicians. You know many yourself who will tell you that always being on the right side is not the most comfortable! It's TRUE! Not all of us use the right half of our brains to its greatest advantage, and that is why I firmly believe the human lefts are on the move!

In our family, the human left factor has quite a strong following. I'm left-handed, as is our son, our daughter-in-law, my cousin, several uncles and aunts. The rights are holding their own for now, but we're waiting to see if the Perfect Grand-daughter will also be of the left persuasion. Get the group of us in a kitchen together and it's downright dangerous. Knives are never where you expect to find them, and a "lefty" using a carving knife next to a right handed person looks mighty awkward. Potato peelers wielded with the left hand don't work all that well either. The cutting edge makes it so the peeler has to be used like a whittling knife. That's not the most controlled method of peeling anything larger than an apple, let me tell you. The most frustrating item is a bread-cutting knife with a guide on it. Unless it's set up for a lefty, it will result in wobbly slices not worthy of peanut butter.

The human rights advocates will scoff as we dash for the dining table all determined to have the "left-hand end". What a relief to be at a dinner party where six of eight in the group were left-handed! We didn't have to worry about drinking from the wrong glass* (*see below*) as our tablemate had done likewise. We didn't have to worry about knocking our neighbour's food off his fork with our elbow either, as we were all eating with the same hand. At last, a dinner party with no major faux pas.

The human lefts of the world also have difficulty when it comes to finding standard implements such as scissors. There are specifically labelled left-hand scissors, but buyer beware: often the handles will accommodate a lefty, but the blades are not reversed, so the darn things are no better than useless. We learn to adapt to larger tools, like the band saw, and in fact would find it doubly awkward if having used that tool in our own fashion, it were turned around for us. Alan can hardly bear to watch me use the power tools. It's bad enough when I use a regular hammer or handsaw. Guess I won't try the chain saw.

There are other issues for which the human rights group has little understanding. Cords on electric appliances are usually set so no matter what we are trying to do, the cord is in our way. I have ironed over mine so often it is permanently disfigured. The cord on my hand mixer always trails through the batter, a nice mess for sure. Trying to manipulate that tiny pointer on my computer mouse with my right hand is like trying to thread a needle while wearing oven mitts. The clickers are on the wrong side for us poor lefties.

My sister taught me the very best etiquette rule that you can take to your next banquet where one place setting is right next to the other. "Ya eats from the left and drinks from the right." Works every time. No more fighting over the bread plate with the tasty dry roll.

We are used to being derided for our less than graceful performance on occasion, but it is not entirely our fault. The bank is a case in point. Try writing your signature with your left hand when the pens are always firmly chained to the right of the counter. (Why does the bank loan millions on the strength of a signature, but chain down the dollar pens?) Try using the debit machines with the little barricades on the left side. No room for left working fingers there!

I was blessed with a mom and teachers who understood my absolute leftness. My mom even learned to knit left-handed so she could teach me. My teachers were left-handed themselves and recognized that a little six year old was not a mirror writer at all, merely copying what she saw others doing. My dad got me a special gold-nib pen so that I didn't have to fight with the old stiff thing that splurted ink over everything I wrote. They did their best to make life easier while I was learning things.

So you see, we human lefts have learned to adapt very well in the world of human rights, and, although we may not always do a task in what looks to others as the most efficient manner, we get the job done. There are a lot of us out here. We're the creative thinkers, the folks who know how to cope with life's little aggravations, like all this stuff that right-handers have invented.

Do I advocate for human rights? Well, sure I do. Human rights, senior's rights, and men's rights too. In fact, there's one Human Right who will always be really important to me. He celebrates his birthday March 1, and I look forward to being on his left. Happy Birthday, Alan.

It'll come up again, so I'd better explain that Mecca of shopping, The Hub. It's our community recycling store, started more than 30 years ago by a determined group of women to support the Childrens' Hospital. Although the initial goal was met long ago, the store continues to support a variety of causes from education to food banks to fire victims. Besides being a wonderful place to find a bargain, it is a restful spot to meet a friend or get to know the workings of the town. Almonte's Hub is duplicated in every small town, and you'd be doing yourself a favour by always looking for that special store tucked into a little corner on the main street.

A MONTH OF SUNDAYS

My mother had an expression to cover every situation: "Don't waste a good worry", "a good attempt beats a bad result", "left-handed is all right". When someone would declare, "I'm too old to start something", she'd say, "And how old will you be if you don't try it?"

Now, here's one that caused us pause: "Why, Edna, I haven't seen you in a month of Sundays!" Was that four Sundays? Or was it thirty Sundays? Was it just a long time, but not a year, or what?!? After much thought, we decided it had to be one Sunday for every day of your typical month.

Winter is often long and it's easy to succumb to the ennui of nothing to do. With that in mind, I'm preparing a list, thirty Sundays long. It'll be eight months of great things to do, most close to home, and BONUS! most for free. So here we go. Use it, change it, try your own activities. Just don't languish when life is to be savoured.

March Sundays we'll embrace our weather. Walk along the river in Almonte, Blakeney, Perth, or anywhere there is a water fall. Have you ever seen ice like that? For real entertainment, buy a little camera, and click off a few pictures. You'll see microcosms you've missed before. Snowbanks, bent trees, old trucks abandoned by the road, people in winter gear. Kids love those little cameras. Don't forget to develop the pictures though, because we might want to re-visit those spots later.

Remember when you were at camp and you made "s'mores", those gooey marshmallow and graham cracker cookies? You can do those in your microwave. Put one marshmallow on a graham cracker, give it thirty seconds on high, and plop another cracker on top. You'll never eat just one. You can have a picnic with these, hot chocolate, and a good story book. I don't care that your "kid" days are long past. Try it, lace the hot chocolate with…whatever. Jazz up the marshmallows with a maraschino cherry. Or roast it camp-fashion in your woodstove. Have to cut a proper stick first though!

Along about the middle of March, the snow may be starting to melt. Get out the rubber boots and a good shovel, and make little rivers along the edge of the street or the driveway. Don't try to be Mother Nature here, just get those little creeks running. If you're over ten, do it in a serious fashion, as if it's a real necessity! My husband has a handy chipper he bought just for this sport.

When you pass the seed display at the local hardware, look for a packet of marigolds. (This display is my undoing! There's no such thing as "buy one".) Plant the seeds in anything that will hold about three inches of soil. A full sunny window will get you blooms before you know it.

This one is actually for a Saturday. Take a trip to your local second-hand shop. The Hub in Almonte is a dandy. Don't leave without a treasure. Check out the toys, the old records - even just for the covers - the books, and the clothes. The Hub has an ongoing auction that begs to have your bids.

Take a country drive. Just head out of town, take the first left, then the first right, then the next left, right again, etc. A map helps, but spoils the excitement. Should take that camera along too, just in case you pass the place with the fence made out of farm implements, or the cows soaking up the spring air, or the wild turkeys. Now, if you come across a little town, go to the store and get a treat. Be sure to introduce yourself to someone too. He just might know your cousin!

Have a dinner party. Invite four friends you haven't seen in, well, a month of Sundays. You can make any kind of comfort food, but here's a treat: Stay Abed Stew. Cut up all the raw ingredients: meat, potatoes, carrots, onions, peppers, celery, etc. Mix in a big Dutch oven or roaster. Pour a can of tomato soup and a can of water (or red wine) over the whole thing. Put the lid on, set the oven at 300 and about five hours later you will have a stew to die for! Now let everyone else add the "fixin's". Light a few candles, put on some CDs, and enjoy each other's company. For sure, they'll all declare you should get together again, ensuring another Sunday taken care of!

Prune your fruit trees. Bring the branches inside and put them in a bucket of warm water for a few hours. Now put them in a large vase, and with any luck they will bloom. Glorious spring! No trees? Check the sunrise and sunset time every day for a week. The days are getting noticeably longer.

So there you have some ideas to start you thinking. I know you're inventive enough to think up a list of your own - there's a task in itself! In no time at all, the month of Sundays will whiz past.

Ah, the luxuriance of a greenhouse! Every spring I have the urge to work in the soft fragrant soil while the garden rests under snow. I can't keep away even when the plants are just poking through, tiny promises of summer beauty. I go on the premise of seeing the new stock, but really it's to get my greenhouse fix. Don't ever bargain for bedding plants. It's hard work, and the greenhouse owners deserve to make an honest living. The plants may be small, but the effort to get them there is HUGE!

HOW I WANT TO BE PAID

We have started our rounds of the garden shops and art shows. Our wallets are already lighter as we have happily acquired a fabulous rooster made of motor cycle and circular saw parts - oh, you'll have to see him, he's a majestic beauty - and a brilliant wall-hanging we've wanted for two years. Of course, we chatted with both the artists, and I discovered we shared a surprising bond.

I have run successful businesses for thirty years, spending hours at my sewing machine making everything from wedding dresses to sweat pants. Thousands of garments have passed through my hands, and always I come to the uncomfortable moment: the exchange of money for goods. Worse is the dreaded question: "How much do I owe you?" I fear I'm over-charging if they really like the item, and often wish my clients would just drop the cheque in the mail, or slip it under the door. I cannot tell you how many times I've laboured over a tough task, only to have my client praise my work, love the fit, and thank me profusely. Invariably, I cut my intended price! Both the artists we met described the same scenario!

Putting a price on one's work is like trying to value one's own children. Once I made fifteen beautiful winsome Holly Hobby dolls to sell at a local craft store. Late in the evening I drove past the shop, saw my babies smiling at me from the darkened window, and was at the store the next morning before it opened to take them back home.

I gave them all away, negating weeks of work, but content in the knowledge that each was loved by a little girl. My Christmas spending money dissolved in a moment of sentiment.

I have worked for wages when I counted each hour as a dollar earned. The work was hardly satisfying, but the pay was adequate. I was not always happy. When the work was pleasant and I knew I had contributed to a success, I didn't even think of the pay, enjoying the effort of a good day's achievement, which mattered a lot more than the dollars.

I enjoy my sewing business and recognize that my clients value my work by paying for it. My teaching jobs are the same. I enjoy the challenge, the daily contacts, and appreciate the money I make from this work. The fact that these clients are also my friends makes my tasks even better. Furthermore, they always add their personal thanks and often pass my name on to others, an endorsement I treasure.

However, my true calling is as a volunteer. I can work just because I want to and suddenly the money issue dissolves into thin air. Furthermore, being a volunteer supplies value beyond any amount of money I might earn. In the first place, I love my free work. Right now I'm luxuriating in a commercial greenhouse, playing in the soil, watching tiny plants burst into bloom, helping our customers choose the very finest plants for their gardens. I haul hoses, clip deadheads, cart hanging baskets, shovel soil. However, every morning I throw open the doors on our warm indoor paradise, and consider myself just the very luckiest. Often I don't get home till long past time, but every day I'm so happy to be there. In the second place, I do get "my money's worth". My customers have come back numerous times to get my advice and report on our successes. As well, my employers treat me like family, sending me home with some pretty nice plants too. They have told me how much my work means to their success, and that fills me with a sense of achievement no pay envelope can duplicate.

My work at The Hub affords me the same satisfaction. One happy shopper, a pleasant afternoon with friends contributing to the welfare of our community, a shared laugh, and above all, the certain knowledge that we are working toward a greater good, are all the pay I need to keep me coming back. Would I do it for pay? I'd have to think about that.

I often try to think what my time is worth. I can't tell you how many times I have told others, " Don't undervalue yourself and your work," or "You should be charging more", when I have done the very same thing. Most professionals know their dollar value: lawyers charge a set fee, so do accountants, but someone else usually sets it, right? I have trouble doing that. Cash is good, no doubt, but I want to be paid in other ways too.

I want to feel personal satisfaction for a job that I have done simply for the joy of effort. If actual pay comes too, then that is a bonus. I want my work to be recognized, be it a simple thank you, a note, or a compliment. I want to be asked to do the job again because I did it well. I want to learn from my experience, and increase my own expertise. And above all I want my good work to reflect in others and encourage them to grow and flourish too.

Now, consider this: how do we deal with paying others, the people who serve us daily, the ones to whom we owe not only money but also gratitude? Be glad to remunerate for fair work value or for a person's artistic talent, but add your own touch of kindness. Don't hesitate to tell your children, your spouse, your employees, or your friends that you appreciate their endeavours. Give them kind words, even if it's for something for which you've paid mightily. A phone call, a note, a surprise gift, will brighten a person's day, and put gladness to cherish in someone's heart. Give someone you love a hug, say thanks often and really mean it. We can accomplish wonderful things when we pass along our best to others. Money will most surely be spent, but kindness expressed sincerely will warm our spirits for a much longer time.

In a marvelous example of the "mighty pen," this article was instrumental in keeping the price of ice cream under control in Almonte for a whole summer! You can bet we "shopped locally" when we discovered that.

THE THEORY OF RELATIVITY

Albert Einstein died fifty years ago, and I'm none the wiser about that e=mc² thing. I'm as close to being a physicist as he was to being a dressmaker. His theory of relativity is lost on me, but then he likely couldn't sew a hem either. We all have our talents, right?

It occurred to me when I heard mention that life in general is going "upscale" that I must having been waiting for the bus when I should have been at the train station, because I'm not seeing this upscale trend in my life. I just know twenty dollars doesn't last like it used to. Apparently it's all relative to inflation and other nefarious things. At least, that's the theory. However, my theory is that the value of money is relative to my "want" and "need" mood of the moment. If I "need" a thing badly enough, I'll pay, but perhaps reluctantly. If I "want" a thing, though, I get busy and talk myself into spending the money with only a mild case of guilt.

Oh, I've been less than prudent at times. I'd not hesitate to pay $20.00 for a garden plant, on the assumption that it will be there for many years. On the other hand, I balk at paying that vast sum for a T-shirt. But consider, I'm wearing shirts I got ten years ago, and they still look all right. The darn plant didn't make it through the first season. Relative value: the T-shirt wins hands down. Where's the sense, I ask you?

We complain about the cost of gas at 80 cents a litre, but will lay out $1.25 for a cup of coffee we could have made at home for a fraction of the cost. Bottled water is $1.50 for a half litre, while milk is $1.30 for a full litre. We line up for the former; we complain when the farmer wants even one more cent per litre for his product. Do I need to bang the message home?

Recently we were at a beautiful art exhibition. Few pieces were priced under $100.00, but buyers were laying down the cash with seemingly little hesitation. They were willing to pay that price for art, a good sign of the upscale trend. To value culture in our midst is an essential part of civility. I suspect these buyers are the ones shopping in the Vintages section of the liquor store and the designer shops on Sussex. Relative to their high salaries, the cost of the art was minimal for them. But wait: I met a couple of friends who bought a particular piece, even though they both knew they could hardly afford it. They will get their money's worth many times over, since their money does not come so easily.

We find there is a breaking point on pricing, and that enters into the relativity theory too. For instance, we will go as high as $4.00 for two ice cream cones, but when it hits $5.00, count us out. I don't care if it is banana flavour; I'm not paying that. Nothing embarrasses Alan more than when we go out shopping and after much dithering I choose an article. Then standing at the cash, I realize it is over the top, and leave without it. I've been known to leave a restaurant after being seated and looking at the menu prices. I have no compunction about saying to all and sundry, "Sorry, you are charging too much for that!"

The hardware store will get me every time. Consider the price of a single bolt securely packaged in fingernail-breaking plastic. Don't tell me every one is hand-made. No, they are popped out by the millions in some noisy old factory for a fraction of a cent each. I suppose the same principle applies to the drug industry as they churn out billions of ordinary pills packaged in the little bottles stuffed half full of cotton. How much of the price is bottle and how much is medication? Relative to the size of the emergency, we will pay dearly for both these items. We don't spend a lot of time bargain shopping when the sink is overflowing, giving us the headache the pills will cure! It still irks me, though.

Don't think I condone dropping vast sums on frivolity with no thought as to the inherent value. For example, would I spend $20.00 on a CD or on a lunch? I'll think about the CD for weeks, likely even while I'm eating the lunch, and then decide it's too expensive. The lunch is long gone; I could have been enjoying the CD for years. However, I needed the lunch, and only wanted the CD. For the most part, we keep the two factors in some semblance of balance. "Easy come, easy go" has never been part of our spending philosophy, and I can't see us revising that even if we were to win the lottery. Oh, all right, maybe for a day or two!

For now, it'll be a frosty morn in May that I plunk down some exorbitant amount without considering the alternatives. So next time we step up to buy ice cream and the sign says $2.50 a cone, I'll be going away empty handed. The theory of "want" related to "need" will clash with common sense, and I'll be leaving empty-handed.

There, Mr. Einstein, how's that for a theory of relativity?

Do pause to consider this ever-so-genteel poem for May, with a slight paraphrase for propriety,

A SONG FOR MAY
Hurray, hurray,
The first of May,
Outdoor lusting
Starts today.

What a grand way to start the summer!

I sometimes wonder if new employees are given any direction on how to treat the public. Well, let me tell you, I could hand out a good bit of advice, the crux of which would be that every customer deserves to be treated as you would treat your own mother on her best dress-up days. Being a clerk is a privilege that comes with a monetary reward, something many clerks would do well to remember when they are feeling bored or put-upon by customers.

THEY ALSO SERVE…

"They also serve who only stand and wait."
Grab hold of the saddle and keep a hand on the reins; I'm on my high horse and it's going to be a fast ride.

If the above quote is right, then we're candidates for the service award, as lately that seems to be what we are doing - waiting. The term "Customer Service" is touted by big companies so frequently that it sounds like a mantra. However, it is often slow in coming. For several months I have been on the phone once a week with two different companies in Ottawa for simple repairs. One finally arrived Saturday, only to tell me if I'd called a couple of months ago, he could have done something!!! He tried a fast fix, left us with finishing to do, scratched our brand new paint job, AND charged us plenty. He was a pleasant guy, though, and after all, he had come. As for the second repair job, I'm resorting to letters, not e-mail either, but lick-the-stamp real letters. We'll see what happens.

Last week I went into what had been one of my favourite little shops, finding a perfect gift for my sister. However, the clerk carried on a phone conversation the whole time he waited on me so I couldn't ask him about a more expensive item in the store. His conversation wasn't even in a language I could understand so who knows what tidbit of information we might have shared? I handed over my money, but didn't deem to interrupt his conversation when he shoved my change across the counter. I snatched up the bag and left, with a list of "should have said's" as long as your arm. I won't be darkening that door again soon!

Ice cream served up by a gum-chewing lackadaisical teenager can sour an afternoon's treat quicker than you can say "triple chocolate fudge." Then there's the waiter who plunks down a meal without a pleasant smile, the gas jockey whom you wouldn't dare ask to check the oil, the clerk who leaves you standing, money in hand, while he chats with the other cashiers. They all make me feel I have no business interrupting their precious time with my mundane need. Here's news for you: I don't have to shop in your establishment; there are many other places just waiting for my money! That's where I'm going, and I don't give a darn if you're out of a job before the week's out.

Now, I understand that wages are often not the best, but a little is better than none. The same goes for service. We are ever so grateful for a simple word of greeting or gratitude that we have made a purchase. And of course, promptness is a bonus. How much effort does it take to smile once in a while, and treat the customer with deference? For many shoppers, the service person is their only contact with the world at large. A cheerful word, a smile, and a genuine or even feigned love of the job will go far in expanding the reputation of the company that is paying the wages. Conversely, wouldn't it be a miracle if that service person gained some recognition for showing enthusiasm that just might lead to a raise?

The clerks and waiters of the world ARE the companies for whom they work. They are more powerful than the managers, the presidents, the shareholders, since they are the ones who come face to face with the consumer dollars on a daily basis. They are the people who keep the customers coming back. Every customer should be treated as if he were the finest customer to walk through the door. That goes for the first person of the day to the last. And even if every person all day takes time to dally over the ice cream flavours or needs a size that's in the back, that one purchase is the one that counts the most.

Consumers will always return to merchants who treat them well. The cost may be a little more, but the good service is worth every penny. The relationship and trust in the market place is what steers our economy, so service people, LISTEN UP! We won't be coming back if you don't treat us with the respect we deserve.

Whoa, Nelly!
You can climb down now.

What's a good book without a recipe along the way? This one could change your kitchen habits forever. Don't be frightened off by the length; just keep reading and follow along. Life's a journey; this is a pleasant side-road!

YEAST MAKES EVERYTHING RISE.

Do you remember that kid's joke, "Why does the sun rise in the east?" "Yeast makes everything rise!" It's corny, but if you're in Grade Three, it's pretty funny. I love working with yeast. For thirty-five years I made bread once a week, four loaves of white, and four of brown. That ended when Baker Bob opened up shop!

There is real satisfaction in making bread: the feel of the dough, the wonderful aroma in the house, to say nothing of the magic power of the yeast itself. So I'm going to share this moment of domesticity with you. Wait, this isn't rocket science. It's just a pleasant way to spend one of those cold, slushy days that March brings. This is an activity for kids too, so haul out the little stool and let them help. You can start at noon and be eating fresh bread at supper.

Take a quick walk to the health food store to buy a good-sized bag of whole-wheat flour, the stone-ground kind, and a little bag of baker's dry yeast. You're going to need two tablespoons of it, not a whole lot unless you get addicted to this - or your family demands it again.

Get out your great big mixing bowl and a wooden spoon, a measuring cup and spoons. Into the bowl put 5 cups of hot water. Add two tablespoons of salt, and a cup of brown sugar. (This can be all sugar, or sugar and molasses, or sugar and real maple sugar.) Plop in a half cup of shortening, a good handful of wheat bran, or oatmeal, or Red River Cereal, or some of each, and mix that all up. Now, the fun part, the yeast. Bear in mind that yeast is a living thing, not unlike those seahorse dealies we used to get from comic books. You have to be nice to it or it will sulk. So, measure out a half cup of lukewarm water

22

in a little bowl, and gently sprinkle two level tablespoons of yeast over the top. Set it someplace cozy, the top of the stove, but not where it will heat up and die. If you want to add a thrill to this, sprinkle a few grains of sugar on the top and see what happens. Kids love this!

When the mix in the big bowl has cooled a bit, you can start to add the whole-wheat flour. It'll take about six cups, and by golly, your arm will get a workout beating that, but persevere! Add a cup of white flour too. When the yeast is all soft and likely has risen a bit, add it to the flour mix. Just make sure the mix is only warm and not hot. Don't want to surprise the poor yeast.

Now you start to add more white flour, a cup at a time, until you abandon the spoon and mix it with your hand. The dough is starting to form up and the yeast is doing its thing. You likely will have to add about five cups of white flour, but for heaven's sake, don't put it all in at once, since some days it only requires four cups and some days more. The dough should be soft enough to work and maybe even a little sticky but not a gloppy mess.

When you can form the dough into a soft ball, sprinkle some flour on your counter, and turn the dough out on it. Now you're going to find out if you need to join the gym and work on arm muscles. Set the timer for eight minutes, and start to knead the dough. Fold it over on itself and push it away from you. Get a rhythm going - turn, fold, push, turn, fold, push, turning the ball a quarter turn each time. Your hands may get sticky or the dough will stick to the counter, so just keep dusting on the flour. When you're near exhaustion and the dough is a lovely shiny ball with tiny air pockets under the surface, you are done! Clean out your big bowl, and wipe it with a bit of olive oil. Plop the ball head first into the bowl, and turn it over. Rinse a dish towel in warm water and wring it out well. Cover the resting dough and set it in a warm spot to start to grow.

At this point you have about an hour and a half to contemplate what is going to go well with fresh bread for supper. We like a big pot of soup, a good chowder maybe, and you can start on that now. Oh, your kitchen is starting to smell divine. You could also take the dog out or make a fast run to the store or wash your hair or whatever, but the soup is the best plan. You're being domestic today, so you might as well go all the way!

When you peek under the towel and see the dough has risen to double its original size, you're more than halfway there. Plunge your fingers into the centre; the air will escape and the ball will deflate. Treat it gently still, turn it out on the counter, cut the ball in four sections and shape them into small balls, getting out most of the air. Let it rest again to regain its composure while you find four loaf pans. Use whatever you have, loaf pans, round cake tins, even a pie plate. Give them a good rub with either shortening or olive oil, and one by one, shape the loaves to fit your containers. Little buns are fun for kids to do. You take a little wad of dough and kind of stretch the dough smooth and pinch it at the bottom. Really, who will care about the shape when they are going to taste so darn good?

Set the pans back in their warm spot and again cover their little heads with the damp tea towel for about an hour. In the meantime, that soup should be more than a concept and actually on its way to the pot.

When the loaves are about double in size, heat the oven to 375. Pop the little darlings in when the oven is hot, making sure the pans don't touch each other. Sit back and wait. Oh, the smell is beyond heavenly! After about forty minutes, tap the top of a loaf; it should sound hollow and be a lovely brown. Turn the loaves out to cool, and just see if you can wait till supper to cut off the heel and swipe it with melting butter!

This whole process takes only thirty minutes actual time. There's just a lot of waiting while the dough rises, so don't tell me you don't have time to try this. It's fun, and ever so satisfying. It's another of those things our grandmothers did on a regular basis. It's another link to a time gone too quickly past when bread was something to be cherished instead of a hunk of chewy white paste.

Just do it. Your grandmother would be proud of you, and oh my, you will wow the neighbours when they smell the goodness coming out of your kitchen. Besides, your kids will be ever so impressed with the magic of yeast.

P.S. You can halve this recipe, but remember - one of the loaves will be gone by supper.

We of a certain age are all too familiar with the following scenario. Mother Nature not only abhors a vacuum, she also abhors the notion that retired people should have free time. She'd much rather see us awash in activities that keep us young of heart, if not of body, and certainly busy.

BEWARE THE AGM

We've passed the Ides of March with no stampede of Romans charging into the Forum; however, we are now into the season of the Annual General Meetings, a season which volunteers should approach with due caution.

Be on the alert!! The first thing a group does to lure in recruits is to feed them very well, and keep on promising gargantuan potlucks worthy of the Chateau Laurier. Case in point: there can be no finer spread than that put on by The Hub members. We sipped punch which I'm sure contains mind-altering soothers. We dined on casseroles and desserts that sent us back for seconds. Then, lulled with bounty of goodness, we got down to the serious business at hand - the Annual General Meeting. To prove how soporific it all was, we passed a new governing bylaw without hesitation or dissent, we elected a new executive without campaign speeches or ballots, we made several generous donations, clapped enthusiastically, and tottered off home.

On awakening the following morning, we realized what we'd done. We'd signed up for committees, we'd taken on tasks, and we'd once again fallen victim to the sacred phrases well rehearsed by every president we've ever met. "The job is easy. You'll be good at it." And once again, we found ourselves unable to even breathe the operative word, "NO!" What to do, what to do? The same thing we did last year: throw ourselves into volunteer work with renewed vigour and enthusiasm.

To avoid this situation, a recruit has to listen carefully. The first phrase, after "We're so glad to have you join us tonight", is

"So…what special skills do you have?" You can bet there are several people reading your name-tag right now. Vagueness won't work either, since just by showing up you've proven an interest in the group. If you pay your membership on the spot, and venture an opinion on a subject, especially one in which you are knowledgeable, you are instantly viewed as a "resource person". Here you go!

Try as you might to stay on the fringes, sooner or later a committee chairman is going to come looking for you. "Can you give us just an hour a week to sort donations?" Silly you; that's one hour there, one hour travel time, one hour socializing time, and there's your morning gone. Never mind that you've met a whole slew of new people, never mind that you actually had a good time, never mind that you're contributing to a good cause.

Of course, there are still the potlucks and socials to attend, always with a special something fresh from the oven. But then, you can whip that up as soon as you get home from your earlier "hour". Don't eat for a day before these feasts. And don't let your guard down once you're there. You know what's going to happen!

Be extra careful at the socials. It's not easy to say no when your mouth is full of the president's yummy chicken divan. There she stands, pleading with you to take up a paintbrush for an afternoon to freshen the place. "Bring lunch, it'll be so much fun." And what do you know - it is! It will take more than the original hour but now you are really IN.

I swear presidents and chairmen could sell snowmen in the Sahara. "You are the perfect person to do this." "It's a really easy job." "We'll get someone to help you." There's not a person in the world could turn down a woeful looking, desperate executive member when the case is put like that. All right now, you've filled that hour, you've made the casserole, you've wielded the paintbrush, and you're now on the phone committee or whatever. That must surely be all.

But no, here comes the nominating committee, just in time for the Annual General Meeting again. Since you now are such a valuable part of the group and have become friends with the various other good souls who work so hard, there are several people pumping for you to be on the executive. Do you see what's going on here? You've graduated! They feel you've succumbed to all the catch phrases so well, you are cognizant of how they work, and are ready to try your wings yourself.

Oh, what a privilege you are being handed. Now you can spend even more time with your favourite group, including evening meetings. Don't take on a major position; just take a committee chair to begin. There will be lots of others to shoulder the load. They must want to do that as they signed up at the AGM, just as you did a year ago. Call the new people first, give them a little task, say an hour a week…

You can do post-graduate courses too. After being a director for a while, you can move up to president. By that time, you will be so dedicated to your group, you will have your own desk, your own post office key. You will be responsible for so much, you will think you're capable of running a major corporation. (You are, too!) Your family will know not to look for you on meeting nights, not to plan their weekends until they see what chore your group has in mind for them. But they will also be proud of you when your picture is in the paper –that is, if they recognize Mom or Dad who now spends an inordinate amount of time with volunteer work.

Does it end? Yes. Will you be sorry? Yes. But there comes a day when you just know you must move on with your own life. Your legacy for your devotion, for just once saying "yes" will be to see your organization thrive and grow. You will always feel part of that wonderful power that only volunteers provide. You will be forever tied to the good works you have done. And years down the line, someone will come up to you and thank you for your time and effort. Someone will be successful because of the encouragement you gave. You will always be able to look back and know your contribution did not go unnoticed. The rewards of volunteer work take a long time to come to fruition, but be assured they do, and you are the richer for it, as is your community.

So don't be afraid of the buffet supper, don't be afraid to say yes, and don't phone me the next morning. I'm at The Hub doing my hour's work. Where are you? We need you! You're the perfect person to...

The only way we're going to make it to "Dancing With the Stars" is if we buy tickets! But we are holding on to the fantasy that maybe one day, if we really practice, we can look good on the dance floor. Either way, we are having a ball learning.

TRIPPING THE LIGHT FANTASTIC

There's a real oxymoron out here in the country. On the one hand guys are "guys", no fancy schmancy girly stuff, eh? Gotta be able to handle a chain saw without risk to life and limb, gotta be able to drive a lawn tractor in a straight line (for those of us who don't have the real McCoy, of course!) Can wear yer work boots and yer hat to any event short of a wedding. Yep, no girly stuff there. However, come to a dance, and by golly, every one of those fellows knows how to swing his partner around the floor for hours on end with every fancy light-footed step invented. And square dance! Well, all this to say, I'm impressed! More than once we have been wallflowers when the fiddlers start into polkas, two-steps and jives.

Now, you'd think people our age would have had plenty of opportunity to learn to dance. We did, way back in high school when it was part of the gym programme. However, all the boys wanted to do was see how hard they could twirl the girls. A few were serious good dancers, and the girls loved being assigned to them, but they were castigated as sissies by the rest of the testosterone crowd, and soon dropped out of sight.

We had regular Saturday night dances, the cruelest event of the week when only the most popular enjoyed the crooning music, and the rest stood on the sidelines willing themselves invisible. A steady boyfriend insured an evening of dancing, but what self-assurance it took for a lone guy to wander over to the bevy of single girls and ask someone to dance! Since it was not "de rigueur" to dance with same-sex partners, both boys and girls endured the lonesome embarrassment with mock smiles and what passed for friendly gossip. Some might have been misfits at those dances, but it would have been a worse faux pas not to attend.

It was during the Robbie Burns Dance a couple of years ago that we realized we were in need of serious dance help, but short of signing up for "Dancing with the Stars", we were at a loss. Then along came the Big Band Dance last spring, and voila, with one simple lesson, we found we could actually do a swing dance not too badly. As long as we kept counting the steps, we managed to make our way to the end of the music without falling in a crumpled mess on the floor.

We were hooked; we wanted more instruction. And that's when we discovered the Tuesday afternoon ballroom dancing class. Now, next to hanging wallpaper, there is nothing to test a relationship like learning to dance together. I don't have to explain that the first problem is who will lead. I guess this is the first time most women have to move backwards and trust their partner to steer in a straight line. Even in a rowboat we can see where we are going while the guy rows. The second problem comes with moving feet so close together. Inevitably, toes will be trodden upon. While the steel-toed boots aren't ballroom attire, they might come in handy once in a while.

Next comes the counting. If you watched our class, you would think we were all involved in polite conversation, but listen: "Slow, slow, quick, quick." "One two three, one two three." " Who's leading, you or me?" "Oh, sorry, I missed that." We even have one step called a conversation step, where we turn to each other and smile, and keep right on counting! We have learned to foxtrot, waltz, and jive, all to the scintillating rhythms of "one two three, etc."

Are we having fun? Oh, you bet we are! Even though most of the men were reluctant to begin these classes, we are all enjoying the experience. Our excellent instructors have infinite patience to get us all going in the right direction. Even the rhythmically challenged are gliding around with confidence. We're no Ginger and Fred yet, but just you wait. We are all proud of our achievements.

Times have sure changed when guys will sign up for ballroom dancing without fear of being labelled a sissy, when girls will dance with each other just for the joy of revelling in the rhythm of good music, when the dance floor can be a source of real pleasure instead of something to be endured for a gym class.

We could all put a little more dance into our lives. Even if we are all alone, we can crank up the tunes, and swing to the sound. In our house it drives the dogs wacky when we do that, but maybe they just want to share in the dance of life too. Will they need lessons?

A sweeping curtsey to our good friend Peter Jones. He danced his way to the end of a full life, savouring the best steps, and swinging us all along with his special joie de vivre.

I GET TOUGH!

I've decided it's time to fire our maid. She's been with us since the day we married forty some years ago.. She's toiled in relative obscurity, rarely letting us down, but lately she and I are having "issues."

When the children were little, she got the beds made first thing in the morning, she did the breakfast dishes, even without the aid of a dishwasher, and kept the living room neat and tidy. Mondays she washed several loads in the wringer machine. She lugged the stuff to the outside line or hung the little things on a collapsible rack over the heat vent. By dinnertime, she'd not only have the clothes folded, but also have a stew ready to set on the table. Never did she leave dishes in the sink in the evenings, never did she leave the kitchen floor sticky, and NEVER, NEVER did I catch her sitting idly in the middle of the afternoon. Even though her day was long and her pay was only the family allowance, she was perfectly happy with her life.

As the kids grew, so did her duties. She took to making us bread every week, yummy cinnamon buns, and cookies galore. The jar on the counter was bottomless. She thought it would be fun to take up sewing in her spare time, and yet she still found time to iron seven shirts a week, and of course, the pillowcases and dish towels too. I didn't mind so much that she started to wash windows only twice a year, since she had gotten her green thumbs into the garden, and was presenting us with canned raspberries, wonderful homemade wine, along with pickles and relishes. She did the ritual spring and fall cleaning, she cleaned the oven, washed curtains, and even painted the little scrapes or nicks that our busy life caused.

All this she did without once bothering to question the value of her work. It was the way it was done, how a home was expected to look, how the preserve cupboard was supposed to be brimming. Every one of us felt comfortable pride in her hard work, especially when some-one commented on it. She blushed easily too!

However, little by little she has been letting her work slip. All right, she is getting to a certain age, and perhaps I shouldn't expect so much. But, really, would you accept windows that reflect long streaks across the floor? Would you accept shirts all perma-pressed, whipped out of the drier so she doesn't have to lift that iron? Would you be happy to open that cookie jar and find crumbs left over from who knows when? I'm even having trouble getting her excited about dusting, which at one time she loved to do.

"Oh," she waves me off, "don't touch the table if you don't want to see the smudge. You can leave your initials but not the date." Dear me, where have her standards gone?!?

The dog tracks mud across the tile, and there she is, just letting the tracks dry, and then sweeping it up! No bucket, no scrubbing, no nagging the dog either. She's taken to bringing delicious bread home from Bob the Baker. She's found excellent jam at the farmer's market. The perma-press shirts are half the price of those expensive cotton ones. And now I hear her on the phone finding some nice young man to come in and wash all those windows in a month. She's perusing the catalogue for a self-cleaning oven, not really a necessity, I think, when she doesn't even use the darn thing so often any more!

She's even winning Alan over to her side. She persuaded him to rent a wood splitter in the fall, relieving him of days of slinging that axe. She's egging him on to develop his acting career, take up woodwork, have some fun things to do. Here's the worst: she's now campaigning for a hot tub!! There goes the whole housework thing.

So, yesterday when I caught her at three in the afternoon, the vacuum cleaner in the middle of the floor, the dog at her feet, and her, there in my chair doing the crossword puzzle, I just had had enough!

"Oh, just be cool." (Imagine the cheek!!) "The housework will be there tomorrow. Just gather the whole thing up and put it away." Can you believe anyone saying that?

Alan doesn't back up my decision to let the maid go. Obviously he hasn't noticed how she's shirking her duties. I think he's getting attached to her. He doesn't complain if meals are helter-skelter; why, he's even taken to making hors d'oeuvres to replace regular meals altogether, excellent ones too.

"Let's keep her," he suggests. "Then every time something isn't perhaps the way we used to do it, we can just blame her."

I tried that this morning. The bed didn't get made until after noon. And I think the newspaper is right where I left it this morning.

"That darn maid is going to have to go. She's getting slovenly again!" I complained.

"I'll help her out," Alan said." She's been here so long, I'd really miss her. Besides, she scratches my back when I need it."

Okay, she can stay, but I'm raising the housework bar, at least to mediocre again. Don't take that to the bank, will you.

Another March, another tune, another threat to a long honeymoon!

NOW IS THE SEASON OF MY DISCONTENT

All those years I was subjected to Shakespeare, I was stumped by the admonition to Julius Caesar about the Ides of March. Well, I finally understand. It's not that someone was going to leap out of the bushes and do him in with a dastardly blade. It was much more devious than that. The true message was that Mrs. Caesar would be gripped by the first stirrings of spring, and want to start renovating and redecorating the palace. In truth, many men might prefer the dastardly blade to being caught in the fury of a women bent on redecorating.

The Ides of March coincides with the sun streaming in through windows at the proper angle to highlight winter detritus, wilted curtains, and that awful airtight dullness of the last few months. I want to throw open the windows and let the fresh air pervade the house. I want to strip down the curtains, wash the walls, shake out the mats, and clean the windows. The dogs better steer clear of my bucket or they will be bathed and fluffed like everything else.

Now is the time I need to peruse what my friend calls the "house porn" magazines. You know the ones I mean: the Martha Stewart specials, the House Beautiful, etc. Certainly not our house at the moment. These glossy fairytales are danger with a capital D. Can you believe the beauty of those exquisite rooms is easily accessible with the mere flick of a paintbrush? They rarely mention the hours of preparation and definitely not the cleanup. Instead they lure us into renewed environs topped up with delicious little beaded cushions and scented candles. The colours are fresh and new, just what is needed at this awkward time of year when drab is no longer an option. It's a wonder a woman doesn't need a note from her husband to even purchase those magazines!

However, most husbands know how to circumvent the domestic crisis looming on the horizon. They head for the hardware store to play with the lawn tractors, barbecues and other spring toys. They hide out near the "guy stuff" in the hopes they won't have to choose between "French flax" and "apple blossom" for the bedroom colour. And for sure, they don't want to get into the wallpaper and wainscoting business. While wives are whipping around choosing brushes and fabric, they are snoozing out in the car enjoying the last peaceful moments before chaos descends on their happy home.

This is spring fever with a passion. It tides us over between the first robin and the lure of the garden. (Actually, it is a precursor to all the plans we have for outside, but don't let the guys in on that one just yet!) What we really want is a fresh start, some colour after the long winter, and the fervent hope that maybe, just maybe, we will attain that pristine room the house magazine promised.

Now, there must be a simple and cheap cure for the seductive call of the Ides of March. Somehow resting till the urge to refurbish passes will not do. Action is the order of the day - we crave change. So the answer is to throw open those windows and wash the curtains for starters. You could get very excited and scrub down the kitchen. You could turf out the winter boot mat and stuff the scarves and mittens in a safe place till next winter. You could spend a full week sanitizing every room in the house, dumping the clutter, washing winter right out the front door.

And then?

You could take a cup of tea out to the porch and watch the melting snow drain down the driveway. You could sit in the sun as it stretches across the front of the house. You could bend close to the warm earth and watch the tiny snowdrop petals unfurl next to a daffodil. You could make a man very happy by not even mentioning the word "paint", much less letting him know that what you really, really want is a full load of topsoil to rework that messy little corner of the garden.

Every year I go through the same planting frenzy. I get to the greenhouse, and even though I know the beds are full, I greedily want it all. Don't make me choose just one colour, one kind; give me geraniums till they spill headily over the edge of the pots, give me petunias crowding every planter, give me daylilies sprawling over the borders. And also give me the strength to straighten up after I've spent the day plunging each little darling into a bare spot. For sure, after a few hours of that, I'm more than happy to share, especially if it'll spare me even one more minute of knee scraping, hole digging, and plant fertilizing.

THE HARDEST LESSON

What little phrase is the hardest to teach a youngster, harder even than the concept of "hurry", which we know you can't teach a tiny person who doesn't even tell time? What do young moms start to say just as Junior begins to entertain ideas of having friends? What have we all self-righteously said, only to have it come back in a storm of tears? Yes, it's "Now dear, you have to SHARE." From the time a little one gets his first favourite toy, Mom exhorts him to give it up at HER will, with the notion that children love to let their favourite thing be mauled by some other wee hands.

When we were old enough to cut a candy bar in half, my sister and I nearly divided the centre molecule, trying to get "the big half", and thus our "fair share." Sharing was not something we did well, and I think we were not alone. Clothes were the next things to be divvied up, and I must admit I was the selfish one there. I should have been smarter - her stuff was definitely better.

We're older now, and both of us are the victims of the pocket-depleting plantaholic disease. I found a mug I should buy her that states, "There are two kinds of plants: mine and those that aren't mine yet." How's that for selfish? Well, I suspect if we admitted it, we should both have that mug, and we'd share, I guarantee.

Gardeners are masters at sharing. We have to be or we'd be buried under foliage! First, ask any gardener to show off his green thumb, and the shovel is quickly tossed for a slow amble around the flowerbeds, noting birds, bugs, blooms, and the occasional weed. The gardener delights in regaling guests with plant sources, compost stories, recipes, and the odd bouquet of fragrance. In addition, most of the knowledge gardeners possess has been gleaned from others. This is especially true if the "Hort Club" is close at hand. Wow, a roomful of plantaholics! Can't you fairly smell the good earth? All afflicted people with garden gloves worn to the threads are welcome to dig right in and feed their addiction. The garden is such a work in progress that we all long to show it off whenever we can. (Don't be shy about asking gardeners to share; they want you to ask!)

Now, this share thing gets even better. When we started our garden eight years ago, we brought a few treasured plants from our last house. They were quickly augmented by a healthy infusion of marvelous perennials from the garden club president, no less. The backbone of our garden took shape. More friends brought us a carload of their best plants to add to our grass garden. The ladies at The Hub contributed a rose bush. Rockery plants arrived from another friend in the City. One year, my mom sent me home with tiny irises wrapped in damp paper towel all the way from B.C. My sister has given me no end of seeds from her garden in Halfmoon Bay, B.C., some of which came from my mom's garden too. And all of these plants thrived and multiplied. So what to do when they've over-grown their space? Why, SHARE, of course. So I've dug up lilies for my neighbours, whacked out irises that have taken over a whole bed, cut up rock plants many times, and sent friends packing with a goodly portion of my favourites. I don't hesitate to share now. It makes me very happy to know that when they walk around their gardens, they think of me, just as I think of the many people who contributed to our flowerbeds.

You'd think I'd stop now that the beds are well and truly full, but that just can't happen. Already Alan and I are planning new beds; already we've made one greenhouse run and come home with little plants to finish off. (If you want to see the most glorious sight, stand half way down a greenhouse in April and behold the plants already pushing forth flowers. There is no finer aroma than moist earth and fresh plants.) As if we don't have enough, we start all sorts of seeds ourselves; what will we ever do with all these tomato plants! I know, I'll give them away. A package of pepper seeds that looked so sparse is now a tray of little darlings that would set up a salsa factory for a year. And sunflowers!! We must have ten varieties on the go. They're tiny now, but wait till August. Did we need so many? Well…maayyybbeee. You can be sure that before the knees are worn out of my jeans as I try to find a corner for every seedling, I'll be quite happy to give some away. I'd never just chuck them, as I want them to have a good home. JUST ASK ME! I'LL SHARE.

There must be a lesson in all this. How's this: when a little child is old enough to dig in the dirt, we give him a full package of seeds, easy ones like beans or peas, and when they grow and he has way more than he wants to plant out, we can encourage him to share, that is, give away something he has carefully grown, something he loves because he has worked hard to nurture, something whose welfare he alone controls. He will be glad to share, and when he realizes the joy that his gift produces, and the fact that he still has all he wants, he will have learned an invaluable lesson, one that will stand him in good stead for the rest of his life. And if in the meantime he also learns that there is no more satisfying pursuit than making our surroundings more beautiful by working in the soil, he will be rich indeed. It humbles us to see the power locked in a tiny seed, and also to see that power multiplied over and over as we send our plants out into the wider world of gardens. Get out that spade and divide your wealth, and may I have just one of those wonderful…….? I've got some…that you'd just love.

We're still new enough to this country lifestyle that we spend innumerable hours cleaning up our forest when we see deadfall. Unlike our garden, which can look, well, all right, overgrown is the operative word, our forest is quite pristine. We are fortunate to have a valuable parkland not a kilometre from here, and when we drive past it daily, we can't bear to see it fouled. The Burntlands is just that: an area that was destroyed by fire years ago, and to this day is relatively denuded of large vegetation. It is an Alvar, a botanical treasure of unique grasses and flowers struggling to grow in limestone and a thin soil. We figure we need to give it all the help we can. You're welcome to walk it and marvel; bring a bag to pick up junk though!

CONFESSIONS OF A GARBAGE PICKER

I'm not actually a "garbage picker", more like a garbage picker-upper. We drive March Road into Almonte just enough to make us think it is our private parkway. Thus, when the snow started to clear, we were disgusted with the detritus left by people intent on transferring the Carp Dump to the side of our road. Honestly, I can't comprehend people who think it is their unassailable right to fling their trash wherever they please. God forbid they should mess up the interior of their precious vehicles with a coffee cup, gum wrapper, or water bottle!

In three hours of collecting five bags of garbage from Burntlands to Golden Line Road we learned a lot about those whom we have labelled "chuckers". First off, they have insatiable thirst. Not only did we collect about a million pop cans, preference Pepsi, but also half full water bottles with lids screwed on. The chuckers don't want to pollute the roadside with bottled water. Strange! Lots of coffee cups, along with milk cartons, juice bottles, and drink boxes make us think that parents are allowing kids to become chuckers too. "Drive and dine" must be the chucker's motto according to all the Subway, McDonald's, and Burger King crap that gets jettisoned with the bottles. Don't want that onion odor fouling the car!

41

Now, the myth that drinking and driving is a thing of the past was not borne out by our pickings. We found 14 beer bottles, eclectic tastes, several vodka bottles, one large Baileys bottle, and a gin bottle in less than two kilometres of road. That doesn't include the innumerable broken beer bottles, which really annoyed me, since we can't cash in broken ones! In general though, I'm impressed with the quality of the beer bottles. Most had been pitched a fair distance, and remained intact. Big points for the glass producers. Add to this collection a myriad of sample liquor bottles, preference Drambuie, and that road begins to look like it is one long moving bar scene.

Alan removed the living art exhibit of plastic floating in the jack pines while gumbooting through muck and stuff on the east side of the ditch. There must be a lot of construction projects with new insulation, vapour barrier, dry wall, carpeting, and shingles according to the old stuff that has been hurled along the wayside. I wonder if the drivers were so intent on wolfing back their fast food and coffee, they failed to see their loads freely departing the back of the truck. It sure cuts down on the cost when they wheel into the dump weigh station if half the junk is left beside the road somewhere. "The garbage fairy stole my stuff."

The ditch was testimony to the hazards of driving too. We came home with a good portion of a poor green Honda that met its demise during the winter. Fenders, trim, mirrors and lights, pieces of hubcap, tires, and a door handle all got left behind. I hope the driver is all right. He sure didn't come looking for the bits and pieces. In fact, there must be many drivers wondering what became of their tail pipes and other oddments. I can attest that they don't rot or rust away. If vehicles lasted as well as these various pieces, we'd not be down at the new car lot every couple of years.

I worry about the health of our drivers too. Many have bad breath considering the number of Dentyne Ice gum wrappers we found. Also, many suffer sore throats and chew copious quantities of lozenges in those dastardly cellpack things that clutter a car if left inside. Best to get rid of those as quickly as possible. Plastic and foil have considerable staying power when hidden in snow or grass, as it was evident some had been there for years.

How could a person lose a glove, a toque or a single sock when they are riding in a vehicle? What about an undershirt? Garbage picking has the makings of some good mystery fiction. We found a few CD's and the inevitable tape glittering in the gravel. Yes, indeed, there is some music that cries out to be yanked from the player and pitched as far as possible. The glove must have come off with the mighty throw. They were lying close together anyway. Further, wouldn't you get a rude surprise when you went to step out of the car with one bare foot? These hapless travellers lead interesting lives.

So, our duty is done, and we are pleased to see our parkway looking a little better for our labours. However, I have to confess we might have to get a bumper sticker that says, "We brake for beer bottles." I'm astonished how many we are finding no matter where we travel. Our kids would faint if they knew their parents were getting their jollies riding around gathering up beer bottles. We're not really losing our marbles; we are just doing our bit to recycle. At least, that's our story and we're sticking to it!

We've never been ones to name our cars or appliances. However, that doesn't preclude my feeling that when the lights are out and we're away, they have personalities that dictate their functioning. The computer is the main culprit, but anything with little programmable chips that control their functions could quite easily be up to no good when we're not around. They all know how to mess with our heads on occasion.

WE'RE WASHING OUR DISHES IN OUR DVD PLAYER

WARNING: *Do not read this in the proximity of a functioning major appliance or automobile.*

We were thinking that we'd leap into the media fray and buy ourselves a DVD player. Our VCR came over on the Mayflower, about the same time as we got our TV. It's a pretty basic model, works all right though, and hurray for me, I even know how to programme the thing. However, a trip to Videoflicks made it evident that if we were to watch anything newer than "Sleepless in Seattle" we were going to need a new system. There were so many neat features on the DVD player and everyone tells us VCR is old hat. We could rationalize ourselves into a new system with no trouble.

Ah yes, TROUBLE! We made the mistake of discussing this new purchase idea in the kitchen right next to the dishwasher. That machine has always been a bit of a problem child, clogging at the least provocation, breaking glasses for no reason, and seizing up when we need it most. So here it was, the week before our neighbourhood party, and we had the audacity to be ignoring it, AND talking about something new and luxurious. Major appliance sulk!! Right then and there, it coiled its wires, packed it in, and died.

Once our washer magician had declared it well and truly deceased, we had to abandon the DVD idea, and start the rounds to find a replacement. This job is worse than buying pantyhose; there are so many brands, features, and prices to consider. The "sales" are on everywhere, which leads me to believe there is no "regular" price on anything. It should have been fun, shopping for a big thing like a dishwasher - or a DVD player which had been the plan if you remember! - but it wasn't. The salesmen (no sales women now that I think of it) knew all the bumf on every one: the water capacity, the number of jets, the big features. And of course, the "sale" was ending Saturday. There was no GST on one, a special discount on another, but no one was willing to bargain. Here was the best though: the one we got, locally I might add, had all the features we wanted, and was reduced on the spot when we said we were "from around here." AND here's the kicker: the salesman, who owned the place, gave us two absolutely delicious steaks!

Wait, I'm not done: when the deliveryman brought the new one, he removed the old one and took it away. Even wiped up the mess on the floor. There wasn't even a delivery charge! That was something we had never encountered before. After eight years, you'd think we'd be used to this wonderful local service, but it still leaves us in awe. We told our city friends our experience; they think we're living in Fantasyland out here. RIGHT!

The sparkling new dishwasher is perfect in every way. We love it. We extol its virtues, and load it with reverence. The prospect of clean dishes has outweighed our need to see movies. All seems in order once again. However, appliances gossip in the dark hours. Not enough we give them a good home. No, they rise in revolt at the first indication one is being favoured over the other.

Good news must travel fast - and far. Not two days after the washer came in, we turned on the tap to a dry sucking noise, and NO WATER. (That translates to no toilet either.) The last one we would have suspected of such treachery would have been our water pump, since it is buried 90 feet beneath the rumblings of other appliances. Our ever-faithful plumber opined it was deep trouble, meaning he was going to pull the pump. We helped him heave 90 feet of wet cold hose and wires along the driveway. At the end was the little pump on which we rely so completely. In what can only be described as fear and trepidation, we awaited the diagnosis, which, praise the Lord, turned out to be frayed wires. (Does he have any idea the power he holds over us and our chequing account?) He spent the better part of a snowy morning tying wires to pipe, and then dropping the pump back down to its cozy quarters. The sound of running water is music, almost of the quality of sound one might find on a DVD player.

How can we second-guess these things? First off, stay clear of advertising that looks tempting. And never, never wander through the appliance centre looking longingly at new stoves, fridges, even kettles. For heavens sake, don't touch!! When you pass a car dealership, pat the dashboard and whisper sweet nothings to your car. Keep it in good repair; wash it occasionally; top up the oil.

Also, don't go gloating over a little found cash. Don't go planning your lottery winnings. You can't outwit these major forces in our lives. All you can do is take it one day at a time, and be happy when everything works as it should. Now, I'm going out to my dear OLD stove and cook up those fantastic steaks, God willing the power stays on!

The TV weatherman declared, "I've got weather for you today, folks!" Being good Canadians, we know that means really big stuff, storms and all, not just your day-to-day atmospheric conditions. We'd have nothing to say if we didn't have weather.

NO RAINY DAY BLUES HERE!

I love a rainy day. It's a great opportunity to play hooky from the outdoor chores of spring and just relax away the day with a good book. Look outside every once in a while and watch the rivulets running along the driveway, see the garden soaking up the water without damaging everything in sight. The cat seems to have the right idea, curled in a white ball on her red blanket. I'm going to make Mom's raisin cookies and put on some fresh coffee and read all day. First I have to make a quick trip to town for raisins, though. Slap, slap windshield wipers, sheets of rain and wind. I'm drenched before I'm in the door.

Home is cozy, and by ten o'clock the spicy aroma of warm cookies fills the house, the coffee is brewing, and I'm getting primed for my rainy day laze-about. I've got the book out, the big coffee mug ready, the milk heated. This is going to be a great day. I snuggle into the chair, get the footstool just right, and here we go. Who cares if it rains for a week? I love a rainy day.

The dog can't comprehend such indolence and keeps sticking her nose under my arm. Well, all right, I'll let you out. Okay, okay, I'll take you out. On with the boots, the jacket, and off we go, rain pouring over my glasses. Can't see where I'm walking, rain is now down my neck, but oh my, she's happy as a duck in mud! I love a rainy day!

After an hour of sloshing through the woods, I need that hot coffee and at least three of those cookies. I shed the wet clothes, which really should be washed now. Might as well stick in a whole load.

But then for sure, that coffee, those cookies, and that book are MINE! There are three phone messages to answer before I pour, though. I love a rainy day.

By now the clothes are ready for the dryer, and I am staring at a muddy floor from the wet boots and the doggy paws. That could do with a wipe-up. Oh, the coffee smells so good, and I'm getting to it right after this. Look at the mess inside this closet: wet jacket, tangle of left-over winter stuff. It'll take but a moment to sort that out. And THEN, coffee and book, here I come! I love a rainy day!

It's close enough to lunch now that there's no point in beginning my lazy day until the soup is heated. That's the very moment the cat over-turns a lamp in her gusto to catch a moth. As I'm lunging for the lamp, the soup boils over. It only takes a half hour to clean the stove, and make a new lunch, but now the coffee is cold, smells kind of burned, and totally unappetizing. I love a rainy day!

The sky is still awash with heavy cloud as the downpour continues, so now I'm really going to throw everything aside and make a pot of tea and READ. Ah, just to relax like this is heavenly! Belle would like a second walk, but she's willing to wait - about ten minutes!! Once more into the breach we go, but this time is different: I'm cold and in a foul mood, not only because we're walking in the rain - and NOT singing, I might add - but also because I'm getting a little impatient with myself for letting all these other activities impinge on what was supposed to be a self-indulgent day. I'm not loving this rainy day quite so much any more!

At precisely three o'clock I am ready to begin the book. I've got the tea, the cookies, dry clothes, and am determined to crack the cover and stay in that one chair till at least five o'clock. Now I can't find the darned book. A futile search leaves me cranky and frustrated. I haven't had the tea, the dog got the cookies, and in fact, I haven't even sat in the chair yet! Alan comes home about four. He's been on a quick trip to the library - to return the books, including MINE!! I'm on the verge of a massive hissy-fit here!!! There goes my rainy day!

Before I can begin my really good sulk, Alan sidetracks me completely with one of those neat little tricks husbands pull off. He's come home with a video, a more than passable bottle of wine, good cheese and our favourite crackers. My original plan has gone completely out the window, but I can hardly stay angry about it. There's no recourse now but to pour the wine, plug in the video and redeem as much of the evening as we can. Before I know it, everything seems to be falling into place: dog and cat are asleep, phone has stopped ringing, kitchen is closed. This does feel good. I love a rainy night when all we can hear is the rush of water and frogs croaking in the pond below the house.

Of all the pieces I have written, this one has drawn the most response. Nostalgia is a powerful thing.

THE CLOTHES LINE

I've never had a house without a clothes line. It was close when we moved to a new subdivision in Dartmouth, N.S., that had aspirations of remaining "upscale" by prohibiting clothes lines. That lasted until we moved in. I insisted on having that metal pole and a long line stretched out the back, didn't care what the neighbours thought, didn't even listen to idle banter about ruining our landscaping. And what do you know, it wasn't long before those metal poles sprang up like dandelions, and we all had a clothes line. Turned out the rest of the community liked the idea, but were nervous about the repercussions should they go against the grain. (We had come from B.C. so I figured we were already against the grain!) On a windy Monday morning we could look down the back yards and see white clothes fluttering like flags of domesticity from one end of the street to the other.

We could tell when our neighbours had extra company (all the towels and sheets), when grandparents were visiting (bloomers and long underwear). We knew when new babies came home (reams of diapers that grew as the child grew). We knew when young folks came home from college (more jeans and sweatshirts). The clothes line provided a commentary on the comings and goings of our friends and reminded us that someone was home in every house. Lack of laundry on a Monday morning was a sure sign of distress, leading us to check on our neighbours. I guess you could say those clothes lines were a sort of lifeline.

I was taught the proper way to hang clothes when I was so short I needed to stand on an apple crate (remember those?) to reach the line. Mom was quite strict as to the order clothes went out: whites first, colours last, rectangular short stuff before long stuff, our blouses before Dad's shirts, and underwear in groups by owner thereof. Socks went last, in pairs and again by owner. This pattern took on nearly religious significance, and Mom would occasionally comment on a woman's ability to housekeep if her clothesline was disorganized. To this day, I have been known to actually remove items I have already hung if they don't conform to the strict order rule. It does make sense though, since it is much easier to fold the clothes and put them away if they are organized from the get-go.

(Oh, an added note: to keep those socks together, pin them before you put them in the wash; no more sorting and losing one!)

Out here in the country, the clothes line is especially welcome. I know one house that always has a few things straining against the wind, even on the coldest days. I admire their owner who has braved plenty to get them out there, all for the joy of smelling that fresh crisp scent when they come in the house. Sometimes the clothes dance like rigid soldiers, other times they twist and turn like fighting fish awaiting release from the constraint of the line.

I love my clothes line. Hanging out the wash on a sunny spring morning is the greatest way to enjoy the first warmth of the season. Once the wash is out, it can be ignored for the rest of the day, while the sun and wind restore the finish. Fresh clothes folded with spring sun warmth tucked inside can't be beat! The summer laundry is a breeze; it hardly gets out before it's dry, but it can still be left all day. Unless, of course, rain threatens. Then it's a mad dash to haul it all in before it's soaked and we have to resort to the dryer. It's a weather game we've all played often. The worst is to be miles from home, see the rain coming, and know the wash is out there.

The winter provides a special challenge. On cold mornings when the clothes freeze as they sit in the basket and the pins are stiff with a touch of frost, the line squeals a protest as I reel it out. This isn't a task for gloved hands, so it has to be done quickly to prevent frost-bite. I make sure the pile is orderly before I go out, since I wouldn't be so particular about the order on a really cold day. Before the last towels are out, the first ones are boards. All day they jiggle and wave in the wind. Just before supper, I haul them in, and surprise! They are often dry. The jeans are a special challenge. I take them off the line and stand them up like a row of "empty" teenagers. A few minutes in the house and they are collapsing in a heap. If towels aren't dry, they get hung where the wonderful winter smell permeates the house.

For centuries women have hung up the laundry, and by completing this simple task I feel tied to the generations of my ancestors who also cared for their families by enduring washday. There is a satisfaction about a neat pile of clean clothes. It's a good start on the week, a fresh supply in the linen closet, a clean slate, so to speak. It provides some order to our daily lives that satisfies me.

Call me crazy, but if I have a choice, my washing goes out in every season. The dryer is only for the emergency stuff or the days when it really is insane to be out there, and we seem to have had our share of those this winter. As long as my line doesn't come crashing down in the wind, which it has done on a couple of occasions, trailing everything into the fish pond, I'll be out there snapping the towels into submission and pinning them to the line. My hands may not be material for the cosmetics ads, but my laundry will have a sweet smell no fabric softener could ever duplicate.

This is a personal tribute to my friend who faced down the dilemma all us seniors know will arrive at some point. There is just no way to make this situation easy, but there is a way to survive.

THE LEMONADE LADY

I'm sure you know the saying, "If God gives you lemons, make lemonade". I have a dear friend who invited me for lunch last week, a delightful quiet repast after a woodsy walk with the dog. We sat in her sun porch completely surrounded by rustling trees, birds, and the occasional squirrel to catch Belle's attention. Anne calls this room her cottage, and indeed the rush of traffic felt a long way off sitting there. She poured our lemonade, and proceeded to tell me about her summer. It hadn't been the best.

Anne has an indomitable spirit. She could find a rainbow in the spray from a leaking pipe! Indeed, I truly believe she is an angel in disguise, a fact she has proven to me and others many times. So often has she shouldered responsibilities and offered aid to her friends that we all see her in a special glow. She is well loved.

Her summer began with a foot problem that kept her from her daily walk (in the last few years, Anne has actually walked the distance of the earth's circumference!!!) Her car is her salvation, and she is a good driver, so she wasn't prevented from her daily rounds of piano lessons, church choir, family and other joys. However, one day in June she had an accident - no injuries, except to her self-confidence. Typical Anne, she was back on the road as soon as possible. But the other shoe fell when her license came up for renewal and she faced the fateful road test. Can you imagine how devastating it was to this dear lady when the examiner, gruff and terse, declared she hadn't looked in the rear-view mirror often enough (every ten seconds, did you know that?!?) and she FAILED?

It took her three days to get over the shock, to finally admit to her family and friends that she no longer had "wheels," and would have to start at square one if she wanted to drive again. Did she resign herself and throw in the keys? No way! She reasoned that if she hadn't passed, she surely needed to rethink her ability on the road. She got a very good senior instructor, who renewed her confidence, and she admitted she did need the course.

Lesson Two of the ordeal came as a bonus. Anne learned that the kindness she had shown to so many was ready to be returned. Her neighbours were nearly lining up to sit as her passenger as she practiced. The only way she could thank them was by asking them again. She discovered that love surrounded her as she valiantly took to the road every day. They all sympathized with her predicament and encouraged her independence.

Lesson Three. When the grandchildren came to visit, they thought they would be housebound, but Anne showed them the whole city on public transport. They were enthralled with the experience, since they'd never ridden the buses. Schedules had to be made, picnics packed, days planned, all so they could go with "Gr'anne" on the BUS. Can you imagine the fun? It was a highlight of Anne's summer. When the children left, she went back to her driving lessons.

Her second attempt at the license was not unlike the first: she was being overly cautious, too slow, not worthy of that prized piece of paper. Again, her neighbours came to her rescue while she persevered through more lessons. The third time to the testing depot they all crossed their fingers, said a silent prayer for this upbeat little lady and waited…

Anne was ready. She needed the morale boost that came in the form of a pleasant young examiner who took her for a little spin. She sailed through the test with no problem. On coming home - alone in her little car - her neighbours gathered in the middle of the street and they all sang and danced. Never was a driver's license as gratefully earned as that one.

Many of us take to the roads in complete confidence that we are indeed qualified to drive. Many are like we are in the country, where without a vehicle we are truly stranded. Although we have neighbours and friends who will help us out, we have to realize that without our car and a measure of independence we could not live where we do. As Anne discovered, we all have something to learn, especially when we are driving in thick traffic. We might be afraid to admit we could use a refresher course, but it can't hurt, can it? I tell you, it doesn't; we did it last year, and discovered that, heaven forbid, we had forgotten things, and no, our reflexes aren't as good as they used to be. So, if you're driving behind me, know I'm seeing you back there every ten seconds; if you're in front of me, know I'm keeping my three-second space. And don't try to pass me and cut me off if I'm only going 90. You're still going to be one car in front of me at the next stop light.

To Anne and others like her, you are my inspiration to see the positive in even the worst situations, and to continue to grow and learn that the goodness that abides with us returns itself in many ways. Anne doesn't want a summer like this again, except for the kids, of course, but as we sipped our soothing lemonade I could tell she'd made the best possible use of the lemons she'd been served. I hope I can do the same when the time comes.

There are times I just can't be quiet about an issue. More than once I've been eating shoe leather because of it, but usually I barrel ahead and say what I'm feeling. You'd think by now I'd have learned about the folly of over reacting, but there are times when I just know it's the correct response. Well, all right, it's a step better than apathy, anyway!

DOING THE RIGHT THING

We've endured the heat of the summer with many complaints, a thrifty use of water, the occasional Popsicle, and blessed Wednesday afternoons at the air-conditioned Hub. Our poor garden looks sadly bedraggled. This week we finally admitted defeat on the "lawn," and dug out the dead grass. We have decided that since the whole area looks like a desert, it can just be one. Yes, we've put in a real desert with cacti, sedums, hens-and-chicks and decorative rocks. It was a bit of a trick to get those prickly plants in place, and we're still extracting thorns, but it actually looks pretty good. More on that as we see how it comes through the winter. We just hope we've done the right thing by not fighting Mother Nature.

This garden has taught us more that once about "doing the right thing." We tried to grow a vegetable patch under a butternut tree. Definitely not the right thing. We tried to make a hosta grow in the sun, again wrong. However, we put a vinca below the spruce trees and that stuff has taken off like a house afire. It's amazing that if we just allow the place to evolve, the plants will let us know what is the right thing.

Life should be so easy, eh? We often second-guess our actions. Responding to a situation in haste leaves us saying, "What if I'd done…instead?" A couple of weeks ago we were driving a rural road in the heat of the day, and there, skirting around the traffic, was the sweetest little border terrier. With no houses in the vicinity, we stopped and gathered the grateful little guy into our car. We drove a fair piece before we got to a house, where the lady told me, "Oh yes, that dog comes from 'way over on the next concession. He's loose all the time, does the whole area." What to do? I guess the heat and exasperation got to me because I let her know in no uncertain terms my opinion of dog owners who don't look after their animals. Poor lady, she got my full wrath, and it wasn't even her dog! I'd burned my bridge then, and before she could take down our licence and call the police, I felt forced to unfasten the leash and set the little fellow free, but I'm not sure I did the right thing. It was what I call an "Irish temper moment". I'm afraid I embarrass Alan when I do that, as he hardly ever blows his stack.

I did it again when the city worker mowed down half our full-flowering meadow along the boulevard. He knew what was coming as I launched myself down the road, probably two feet off the ground in full fury!! I'm not proud of that now, but it sure felt right at the time. I still burn when I see the devastation. We're putting up a sign so that won't happen again!

We are taught at an early age to try to curb our emotions and reactions, and in this age of violence it is even more important that we try to "do the right thing." But honestly, sometimes we need to get passionate about things. This summer, when the Town threatened to cut spending on the childrens' beach programme, a group of moms got their dander up, and plowed into the political sand box to get what they knew they deserved. To their credit, they achieved a marked success. They staged a beach party, they raised awareness, they worked for their kids and their community to keep the programme going as best they could. They understood the importance of swift actions to get the required results.

This sort of energy can be extended. We can all afford to become passionate about things occasionally. It surprises the opposition when we do, especially when they are used to complacency. We need to learn to wade into controversy when we think we can make a difference. Link arms with others of a like mind, and just see the results. The obvious example of that is the efforts of so many in our community to keep our seniors' care facility in the hospital. They want it, they need it, and by golly they are getting it! How can we not want to be part of such a sincere endeavour?

Kids aren't immune to this passion either. Look at the efforts of children to see clean water in Africa or to end child labour in the rug industry. Children often don't see the pitfalls ahead, and are willing to put incredible energies into projects. "Can't" isn't part of the equation. Their passion infects adults too. We would do well to encourage our youth to undertake these giant ideals, since our adult perspective will throw up all sorts of road blocks of which they don't even conceive. Show us the way, kids, and we'll follow! Do the right thing!

When I think back on my two "Irish moments", perhaps I should have apologized, but darn it all, I think I did the right thing on both occasions. I know for sure our boulevard would not now be a mass of yellow and white flowers. I only can hope that the wee dog's owner got a call from the lady I bawled out so severely, and maybe his daily excursions have been curtailed because of my hysterical outburst. I can assure you, should we ever see him on the road again, I'll be doing the right thing when I scoop him up and take him to somewhere safe where an owner won't be so cavalier with a pet.

I know we can't impose our will on everything, but when we are convinced we are right, it is difficult not to go with our instincts. If we think it is the right thing to do, we should act. We should put ourselves into life, not be the ones on the outer ring watching and criticizing. If we never let our emotions come to the surface, who will know our true feelings?

This isn't meant to lay on a guilt trip, but it might open a few memories that deserve to be revisited. You never know what could come of walking back into a peaceful place of contemplation. It sure has given us some good times again.

WHAT TO DO ON SUNDAY

At the bottom of my treasure drawer is an impressive looking lapel pin. The central enameled medallion is surrounded with a gold wreath and below it hang twelve bars. To own one of these pins was a real mark of achievement. I haven't looked at it in years, but that doesn't diminish my pride in owning it. It is the United Church Sunday School pin. I suspect there are other people who also remember the days before Sundays became shopping days when the masses worship at Chapters, Walmart or Starbucks.

It was a kinder, gentler time. Ladies wore hats, little girls had white shoes, and little boys had their hair slicked down clean and neat. We trooped off to Sunday school, not so much with a burning desire to learn religion, but with the expectation of a regular Sunday tradition. I well remember the day my sister declared she wasn't going any more. My dear father nearly had a fit; my mom was totally exasperated, and I was awestruck at Sue's fortitude in the face of such a decision. She never did return, forfeiting the gold pin and the bars. I don't think Mom ever got over the fact that one of her daughters gave up on the United Church and Sunday school.

Over the years while I was at university, I enjoyed going to church, singing the familiar hymns, and feeling a part of a greater whole. When the kids were young, we took them to church and Sunday school. They all had "good clothes", and I even had a hat. We felt this was an essential part of their upbringing, and believed they were happy with the other children, cutting out little churches, learning "Jesus Loves Me", and hearing the familiar old Bible stories. Came the fateful day Steven announced he'd had enough of it when he couldn't colour his church red, and no amount of coaxing could get him back.

By then, Alan was studying every spare moment, so Sunday became the day we'd pack up the family and head off for a picnic or a day in the country. We decided it was more important that we have that time together as a family than be sequestered in a church, us upstairs and the children downstairs at Sunday school. We never did get back to going to church. Our children were raised with good Christian ethics, and they all have a respect for the religious aspects of life. The Golden Rule was a big part of their upbringing, as were the Ten Commandments, although they would likely tell you they were disguised as the One Hundred Mother Commandments.

One of our favourite things to do is drive around the countryside, and once in a while stop at a church graveyard to see the old names. We can imagine the families, the warm communities surrounding those old clapboard or stone churches, the church suppers, the weddings, the christenings, the funerals. Last summer we were privileged to be part of a mini-tour around West Carleton to see several churches in the Diamondview - Torbolton area. One was a dear little stone Presbyterian church called St. Andrew's Kilmaurs. It sits at the corner of Kilmaurs and Woodkilton where once was a thriving community. Now it is alone, with only the remnants of the little town to suggest that at one time it was an important part of the life there.

On a whim one Sunday morning, we took ourselves off to that little church again. The promise of the "Country Sounds" singing ensemble belting out renditions from "Oh Brother, Where Art Thou," seemed like a pretty good bet. We arrived as the group was setting up their sound system. We were greeted with warmth and settled into - yes - a VERY uncomfortable pew. The group shared some good chuckles as they tripped over a nest of wires, shuffled music, and sent someone out to bring in the leader's hymnbook. Then with little fanfare the service began. It turned out the minister was the keyboard player, and a good one he was.

Seventeen in the congregation, five in the singing group, all ages. We sang the songs I remembered, we had a good short sermon, humorous and appropriate, and we listened to rousing songs that made us all clap! After, we stayed for coffee and one of those squares you used to get only when the bridge ladies came over in the afternoon. So good! AND we were invited back the next week when they would be celebrating Heritage Sunday with stories about the founding of the community. That service would be topped off with a beef and ham luncheon. They told us Chester's baked beans are worth coming for, and there would be some thirty pies from which to choose. We didn't think long before we made a return trip, just to test out the beans, and hear those favourite old hymns again.

This got us to thinking. There are any number of churches in our community, all with welcoming congregations that would take in visitors any time they would like to come. What if we were to go to a few over the next while? Churches offer solace in present times, and they exude the spirits of all the people who came years ago with promise of a good future for their families and faith that a greater strength would see them through the rough patches.

So this is what we might do on a Sunday. It won't be a regular occurrence, but I must admit it was comfortable to be there that summer morning. Furthermore, from time to time I'd like to be in the company of others with a similar desire to connect with a higher power. Prayers never come amiss in troubling times. We all could do with a shoulder on which to lean sometimes, and there is no congregation in the area that wouldn't offer one to a new parishioner.

The parting words of the minister at Kilmaurs solidified our intent to return: "Don't be a stranger, eh?" No one would be a stranger once enveloped in that cozy congregation.

One of the rites of summer is berry picking. Since I was short enough that I didn't have to sit amongst the bushes, I've been picking berries: huckleberries, blueberries, strawberries, all to turn into treats for winter eating. We are not alone in this pursuit. I can fairly taste those berries when we see the first signs posted along the roadways. "Pick Your Own" is an invitation too tempting to deny!

REVELATIONS IN THE BERRY PATCH

The season of fruit-bearing bushes is over for another year, and a good season it was, too. The freezer is stocked with strawberries and blueberries, and we had a feast for a week on the raspberries, which are just too precious to consign to the freezer. The ritual of berry picking goes back to our childhood when we hiked up steep green hills in the Kootenays of B.C. to pick the fattest, juiciest huckleberries. On Vancouver Island, we clipped our way into the thickets to emerge scratched but victorious with brimming baskets of succulent blackberries. Nova Scotia yielded blueberry bushes hanging with dusty blue marbles of fruit, free for the backbreaking work of picking. I can't remember a time when summer hasn't meant grabbing the baskets and pails and heading for the berries.

Picking entails a particular etiquette, whether you're in the wilds or in the berry patches laid out in neat rows. It's an activity that crosses all the barriers: women in floppy sun hats, husbands with stools in hand, children who should be weighed on the way in and the way out! All ages are welcome, for even the tiniest fingers can find berries under the greenery. Husbands and wives often start in the same spot, but before long they find their own niche. One picks quickly, one slowly, one chooses only the biggest, one takes every ripe one she can find. Kids have to stay close to the adults, but teenagers are allowed to wander down the rows to their own patch, since, really, you don't want to be seen with your parents doing this job or it's not exotic.

Once you are assigned to a row, the protocol sets in. You must stick to your row and not pick in your neighbour's area, even if your neighbour is your child or spouse. There is no attractive pose for picking; either you are hunkered on a little stool like a milker with a very short cow, or you're bent over like a circus performer with - ahem - not your best profile exposed. However, no one notices, since you're all in the same contortions. Heads down, fingers busy, plick, plick as berries land in the baskets. For a few minutes there is silence, but quiet conversations are inevitable.

"…and when he told me he was leaving, I couldn't believe him."

"…we were in China only ten years, but honestly…"

"… and then he, like, gave me this, like, ring thing for my nose."

It's not eavesdropping because even the softest voices carry, and what else can you do but listen? Also, you never look up, so you don't really know the speakers. That's got to be all right.

When hands are busy, tongues can wag away unabashed, and before long, berry patch conversations begin to overlap the rows. The soap opera story hit a common chord with a single mom with her back to us. A little Chinese girl wanted to know where the lady had lived in China. Only the teenagers gave us pause, as their conversation ran to situations we either didn't believe or didn't want to remember from our own youth. We also realized no advice was wanted, that was a sure thing! They were in their own little world there.

Before long we all have a part of a new conversation. Even the men, who come in for a bit of friendly ribbing, add their voices to the mix. Names are rarely exchanged in the berry patch, except when families are mentioned and one person is the second cousin to "the Smiths who had the cottage on White Lake". Generally, the men seem to just get to work and pick, hoping the ordeal will be over sooner. But when a couple of them get together they launch into topics like fishing or what's going on in town. It's the men who come up with the raunchy little joke that sets everyone off on a good laugh, too. While the women multi-task by talking and picking at the same time, the men are frequently more casual, and when the talk gets good, the picking slows. The social aspect of the patch is equally as important as the work ethic, though, so long as when the time is up, the baskets are full.

Besides the gossip that settles in the rows, there is also a veritable oral cookbook of the best recipes. The lady with the big plastic pails will tell you exactly how to make the best jam and jelly. Ask the woman with the sun hat how to make a decent pie. The guy with the Tilley hat knows what you do to make freezer jam. And the little boy with berries squished around his cherubic face can tell you where he found the fattest, sweetest strawberries to eat right now. No one doubts that these recipes are available on the Web somewhere, but they are more genuine when they come right from the patch.

When the baskets are full, we regret having to leave. Good-byes and good wishes are left with the remaining pickers. Our places are quickly filled by enthusiastic newcomers who welcome the stubby little stools and are soon hunkered down right where we left off. And so it goes. Up and down the rows, this little scenario is played out over and over all day long. No one oversteps the bounds, no one damages the bushes, and no one wastes even one precious berry. We respect the bounty we are privileged to pick as well as the farmer who allows us access to this rich field.

We don't really notice the price we pay for this privilege, since it's come with the added bonus of limitless entertainment. We would never recognize our fellow pickers on the street but for sure, we're going to remember the recipe they shared. In the depth of winter when we thaw out those berries we're going to savour the taste of the day spent picking. We might not recall how hard they were to pick, but we'll sure remember the warmth of the sun on our backs as we did it.

We don't get really dressed up any more, a pity I think. It might have been uncomfortable to be duded out in hats and gloves, but oh my, we did look good for the pictures. Young people in particular have never acquired the knack of formal attire. When they don heels, they can't walk well; the shoes are soon kicked off and ties stuffed into pockets. Hats are out of the question. Oh, to be at Ascot for the races!

ON WEARING A HAT

Not long ago, I bought a new dress and decided I needed a special summer hat to go with it. How pretentious, you say. But a hat makes me feel like a million dollars. Since we were going to a garden party, I thought most likely many ladies and several gentlemen would come in hats. Most definitely all the children would. They are accustomed to wearing the cutest little sunhats now, so for them it's natural. But for us who seldom wear fancy hats, it makes any outfit special. In fact, we all seem to stand taller, take on an elegant look, and move with grace.

When we were young, everyone wore hats. We look back on our wedding forty years ago, and we were all in hats. They were mostly tulle and straw confections, with demure little veils or dainty feathers. Mine was a marshmallow of pink tulle which sat jauntily to one side, and yes, I had pink gloves too. Mom's looked like an inverted petal flower pot, while my sister had a Jackie Kennedy pillbox affair with netting scallops. None of us would be caught dead in those now, but oh my, I do love the aura of elegance a hat lends to an occasion.

I adore hats, and have several, but wear them sparingly, thinking I might look ostentatious. One is a small straw hat with a vibrant yellow flower. That one is a favourite. I wear it in the garden and am astonished how many times the hummingbird has streaked past. It is light and just the right size to ward off the sun when I'm zooming around the yard on the tractor. I can plop it on my head and even with my knees garden dirty I feel like the lady of the manor.

My go-to-market hat is a larger straw hat made in Australia. It sports a big straw bow at the back. I managed to outbid everyone else at the Noreen Young Bursary dinner for this one, which makes it a double treasure. I wear it to the Carp market on Saturdays, or to go into the Big City, or any time I'm wearing a summer dress. I have worn it to church, but take it off before I go in, since I know it's big enough to block a person's view. It can't be plopped on, but needs a moment of adjustment to get the bow just right.

Then I have a blue hat wound round with a flowered silk scarf. That one is squishable so I can travel with it. I call it my painting hat. It has been to France and Germany, and I have a lovely photo of me painting beside a river wearing that hat. I have only to see it to be inspired!

There's a huge black hat with two ochre roses for which I wish I could find an occasion. It is indeed dynamic bordering on the overpowering. It hangs on the wall beside a green hat that belongs on a yacht, the long ties streaming over the starboard rail. A white hat with a burgundy dahlia completes the collection. The latter looked better on the display than it does on me, but the day I bought it I loved it. It gets at least a yearly outing when I wear a matching dress.

Whenever I see people wearing hats, I know they've taken a minute to think of their appearance before they leave the house. Their hats become a fashion statement that says "I care about me." The hat completes the outfit, no matter that it's just shorts and a T-shirt, and lends an air of confidence to the wearer. We should start a movement to see the return of hats as a routine thing like wearing shoes. In fact, there are several women about town who already are on that band-wagon so we only need to climb aboard. Next thing we'll be wanting is a real millinery shop. (Young ladies may have to look that one up in the dictionary!) Now, if I could ditch this bulky purse I'd have an extra hand to hang onto my hat on the windy days. Then I'd really look elegant.

We were approaching our 40th anniversary, and wanted to celebrate in grand style. With family scattered from Germany to Calgary, we knew it would be a stretch for everyone to come, but indeed they all arrived, along with our future in-laws from Germany. For our next big celebration we will go off to some quiet little place and remember what we went through the last time!

"BUNNY'S HAVING A PARTY!"

This was an expression my mom would say when we passed a house with cars lining the driveway. As kids it was a game to spend the next few minutes trying to guess the occasion, who was there, what they were wearing, etc. The best parties were the weddings, when we'd sneak a peak at the bride if we could. It all looked so easy, carefree, and elegant. Little did we know!!

Now we're older and should be much wiser, but that doesn't seem to stop us. In a moment of undoubted insanity I opined that it would be fun if all the family would come for a week in July, if we could invite friends and neighbours and have a real Bunny party of our own. We'd sit around and enjoy everyone's company. Just keep it all very casual, go out for meals, maybe take a couple of day trips with a picnic or something easy. How much work could all this entail?

Since the garden usually looks pretty good then - and the house would be full of family - we could have a little garden party to celebrate our anniversary. A few invitations couldn't be too hard. It would be the holiday weekend, and a lot of people would be away, so it would be manageable. Besides, we had lots of lead time, so the whole thing would be easy. Hey, we might even strive for elegance by hiring a little musical group.

I had this illusion of having all the food in the freezer by mid-June, the house repainted spic and span, the garden all weeded and green, the little tents set up with the chairs freshly cleaned. Why, I stupidly thought I'd even have time to make a new dress. All this depended on doing nothing but party planning for two months, and it's more than obvious my life doesn't even come close to that! Martha has no worries that I might take over her empire.

Time flew past, and suddenly crunch time was upon us! There we were in mid-flight, two weeks before the arrival of ten people. There wasn't even a cookie in the freezer, let alone some fancy baking, and I was trying to figure out how I could prepare food for this elegant "après-midi" with extra people in the kitchen. Furthermore, we were expecting future in-laws from Germany, so everyone had to be ready to don aprons and stir cakes in whatever language they could muster.

We went into overdrive on house maintenance. We cleaned everything, even the basement, for heaven's sake. We painted the kitchen, spruced up the outside trim, scrubbed down the hot tub, washed the curtains, hung new pictures. We should have company more often, if I could stand the pace. Our "To-do" list exhausted us just reading it!

The garden wasn't co-operating the way it should. ("Vanity, vanity, thy name is gardener!!") While we were away for two days, the deer tied on their bibs and ate the phlox and several hostas. Some little critter cleaned off my carrots and Swiss chard as soon as they struggled through the ground. You've never seen anything so pathetic as a garden box with onions around the edge and weedy earth in the centre. I was tempted to stuff in bedding plants and call it mixed gardening. The cucumbers and squash were barely holding their own as each day one more fell victim to cutworms. What should have been an abundance of asparagus was two measly little sprigs, and the dill that should have been all frothy and green sat sulking as two-inch shoots. Never really liked dill anyway!

Consider the lilies, though. They were magnificent, including one small rosy calla lily that took my breath away. I hoped everyone would look past the weeds and enjoy the flowers, the company, and the celebration.

The day arrived, sunny and green, just as we'd hoped it would. The music was idyllic, the food delicious, the drink properly chilled. Everyone strolled through the garden oblivious of the sweat and tears we'd poured into it the previous week. Pictures were taken in abundance, as groups relaxed in the shade. We had a wonderful time, buoyed by the knowledge that we'd done it up right. We were tired, but satisfied that Bunny's party was a success.

So here's what we got for day-dreaming in Technicolor about the perfect après-midi. It was indeed pretty special regardless of the recalcitrant garden: we got the opportunity to have all our family together, something that hasn't happened in many years. We got to enjoy our perfect granddaughter for a few days; we got to share in the planning of the German wedding in September; we got to show off our part of the country to new relatives. We were glad to have the opportunity to introduce our family to our friends, as well. All in all, it was a great "Bunny party." The memories will linger long, and we'll know that for at least a few weeks the house and garden were looking the best we could muster at the time.

Remind me of all this the next time I say, "How hard could it be?" And in August that'll be us with our feet up, relaxing.

THE WOODPILE

What is it about late August? There we were in the midst of the best colour of the summer, the flower beds were lavish, the tomatoes overflowing, and the pumpkins taking over the garden. We should have been relaxing in all this bounty, but no, we were out in the woods evaluating the BTU's of trees! In a little over a week, we took down about thirty trees that had succumbed to the ice storm damage. That sounds easy enough until you consider that from standing in the forest to shoving into the wood stove some time in February, that wood has to be handled nine times.

When we were kids, wood gathering was an adventure. Alan can remember going out to "old Bill Hass's place" for the winter wood. He and his Dad enjoyed this time together doing man work. For a ten-year-old boy, it was heady stuff to use real axes and saws, and be treated like an adult. After they'd filled the back of the old Fargo pickup truck until the rear was dragging, the men would retire to Bill's cabin to drink strong coffee and exchange stories. When the afternoon was nearly gone, they'd roar out of the wood lot, Alan riding on top of the load coming home. I can only imagine what his mom must have thought when they arrived home!

My grandfather conned my sister and me into piling slivery old slab wood. He'd tell us we could only do it as a special treat, and often wouldn't allow us to touch it until we'd gone for the mail or swept off the front porch. (Now I can't believe we were so gullible!) It was cedar and we'd both end up with itchy arms, but oh, we thought we were so smart being able to pile that wood for Papa. Tom Sawyer could have taken lessons from him! My grandmother thought his deception was shameful!

There is something comforting about a neat pile of wood. It's an accomplishment to be able to stack it so it doesn't fall over - an art we really learned only this year. We have stacks out in the forest, we have stacks at the back of the garden, we have stacks in the basement, and they are all different. The ones in the woods are usually propped between trees close to the path. They are round ironwood, so need keepers on the ends. There are three piles close to the house: one waiting to be split, huge things that stay in place on their own accord; split stuff only good for the maple syrup stove in the spring; and the prime stuff split and ready to be loaded into the basement. We take particular pleasure in making that stack neat and tidy, since it is right at the entrance to our forest. Some might say we have too much time on our hands, the way we fuss over these piles, but we consider it a country art to make them look good. We're not real pro's at it yet, but then we've been doing this for only ten years.

This year it was late September when we got to the best part of the job, the splitting. What could be better than going out in the early cool, geese calling, maples red, no bugs? And oh, do I love working the wood splitter! Talk about a power trip, when you smack one of those huge chunks of wood into the splitter, pull the handle and watch that baby go to work! Every five pieces of wood represent a half-day of warmth, so it adds up pretty fast to a warm winter ahead. Never mind that back muscles are screaming at the end of the day, just seeing the pile grow is worth the effort.

Now, the wood business is a country indicator of season that is completely lost on city folk. In August, guys are in Saw City getting the chain saws geared up. You see rough tracks into the bush along country roads, and the whine of the chain saw is heard in the land. In September, Home Depot sells those little plastic stacker ends and great blue tarps. Rental companies put the splitters out front. Big trucks hit the highway with gigantic loads of logs. Ads for firewood pop up in the paper. By October, wood lot owners are in serious delivery mode. Half-tons and pick-ups are loaded till the axles groan with good beech, oak or maple. Piles are dumped at the ends of driveways. A full cord of wood looks bigger than a load of topsoil in the spring! On frosty mornings, thin woodsmoke columns begin to streak skyward all over the valley.

Nearly every country house has a wood stack, some neatly accommodated in a lean-to where every piece is perfectly in place.

Oh, I do admire those piles! I'd love a structure like that, but I wonder if I'd be able to upset the symmetry by removing even one piece. You just know the owner really cares about the appearance of his work. Then there are Down-East piles, those beehive arrangements that aren't as easy to emulate as you'd think. My beehive looked more like an anthill! It took me three years to master the stacks with square ends that are self-supporting. I used to cheat with rebars pounded into the frozen ground, but at last I have created the proper end bits, and so far our stacks are still standing. Our friend the woodcutter tells me they should each be a cord, but I'm just glad to have gotten the principle right. I'm not concerned with the quantity. Besides, I still am not sure about face-cords and full cords, and don't need to go there.

We have brought a goodly amount of wood into the house for those mornings when the house is chilly. I love firing up the woodstove and standing there warming my backside. It's one more opportunity to convince myself that we are in some measure self-sufficient. Our woodpiles may appear to be a ton of work, but it's good for us, and makes us truly appreciate the symbiosis between man and nature. It makes us part of the seasonal landscape, and besides everything else I get the opportunity to use a really big piece of powerful equipment! That's a good thing!

My sister and I were so lucky to have Horace McCoy Keys for a Dad! Of course, we never called him that; to us he was Dad, who made his little girls feel like princesses until the day he passed away.

WHAT I LEARNED FROM MY DAD

Dads have come a long way in a couple of generations. It's common to hear a dad say he's giving up outside activities to devote himself to playing with his new baby. It's the norm to see Dad hanging out laundry, wheeling a little one through the grocery store, or drying tiny daughter tears at a soccer game.

When we were young, dads didn't do stuff like that. They left the child care mostly to the moms. Dads were around to help us learn to ride our bikes, running behind with one finger on the seat while we screamed, "Don't let go, don't let go!" They got together and cleaned our beach so we'd have a place to swim in the summer. They built the playground and field house. But in general, dads were the ones who left for work in the morning, came home tired in the evening, and whom we treated with reverence. Moms, on the other hand, were always there, doling out discipline, hugs, cookies, etc. He taught us to honour our parents.

Our dad was indeed special, and we likely took too much for granted. He worked hard, and desperately wanted a place to relax. With considerable finagling, he managed to get the materials to build us a beautiful little cottage on Kootenay Lake near Nelson, B.C. For us, it was paradise, for him it was a work house! It took constant maintenance, so while we swam, played in the forest, or paddled about in our little boat, Dad was up on the roof cleaning tree limbs, or building a rock wall, or hand digging a well, or worst of all, chasing off the numerous snakes that were lurking everywhere. He was deathly afraid of snakes, but never let on to his two sissy girls! For all of us, our fondest memories had to do with that cabin. He taught us that simple pleasures with family are the best rewards.

Dad had a huge oak roll-top desk that now sits in our home. He "did books" for several small businesses, and always had a radio going. He'd call us down to his office, and we'd sit up on the desk while the radio crackled out "all the way from Salt Lake City" the hilarious adventures of Amos 'n' Andy or Fibber McGee and Molly. I don't remember Mom coming down to listen, but Sue and I thought it was pretty special to share those times with Dad. He loved a good laugh. He taught us the value of entertainment.

One summer we spent with my ailing grandparents in Nakusp, a jewel of a town set on the Arrow Lakes in B.C., Dad borrowed a big old boat with an inboard motor made from a washing machine. He was never good with motors, but kept that thing running pretty well. Every afternoon we'd take off down the lake to a sand bar he knew where we'd swim for an hour or so. Sometimes he'd troll a fish line over the back of the boat on the way home. My worst fear was that we'd catch a fish and it would flop all over the boat. Mom was glad to see it, but Sue and I were scared of fish. I told you we were sissies! Dad made the summer so much fun for us, even though for him it must have been a sad time, knowing his parents were so close to the end. He taught us that nature holds the power to heal.

We had some wonderful vacations. He loved to tent camp, which was an inexpensive way to go in those days. Dad gathered friends for souvenirs, and while we waited patiently for him, he'd he chatting up some old geezer about the history of the area, or who they might have known in common. No matter where we went, Cape Breton, California, didn't matter, he'd find someone with whom he had a connection. He took us to Disneyland, Yellowstone Park where we lunched with bears one day, and San Francisco where we all rode the cable car. He taught us that adventure is necessary for growth.

As we got older, Dad could see his daughters slipping away. He'd look at us with a nostalgic sigh, and I know he must have felt those magic little girl years went all too fast. He'd wait till our boyfriends were taking us out the door to quietly ask, "Do you have a handkerchief? Have you been to the bathroom?" And then laugh fit to choke! The trick was to get the door shut before the last phrase. It's a wonder any boy ever stuck around! He taught us to laugh at ourselves and not take life too seriously.

Dad left life as he had lived it. When we last visited, his breath was laboured, but he could still tell us a joke he'd read in the Reader's Digest, his favourite source of good lines. For the life of me, I can't recall it now, but at the time we laughed so loud the nurse came running to shush us! He loved to read, read to us every night, making us cry over the Ugly Duckling, or shiver over the Wicked Witch, so I read to him Saturday Evening Post stories and mysteries. He taught me that books can be an escape from even those things we don't want to face.

I can sit at his big old desk and its faint aroma brings back a flood of good memories. We were lucky girls to have a father who loved his family so much. On Father's Day I pass the rack of cards with regret that I can't buy one for him and send it off. I still stop and read them though, and when I find a funny one I silently say, "Dad, this one's for you."

There are times when words come out of the blue and hit with such a force that they leave a lasting impression. When these words are graciously said, they leave a kiss on the recipient. And couldn't we all use a few more of those!

THE SUPREME COMPLIMENT

What's a compliment? It's a little sentence that makes your day; it's a major chord in a minor key. We all feel special when one of these gems comes our way. There is one such phrase that can never be taken lightly, and is indeed the epitome of sincerity.

THIS IS MY FRIEND

I heard that introduction over the summer, and since then have been mulling over its import. What higher accolade could one give another than to declare friendship!

When we're little we have "bestest friends in all the world", which usually last until the end of the month or the next birthday party. We toss this title on our pets and our favourite toys of the moment, the things that hold special significance in our lives. There isn't a mom or dad who wouldn't melt as little hands clutch big legs, declaring, "You're my bestest friend." Heady stuff for a toddler and his parent!

Kids don't always make friends easily, but usually when they do they remain friends for life. Paths may divide, but they converge again whenever pals meet, no matter how long the separation. Conversations resume right where they were dropped years before. And oh, how the memories flow! I think this is how it is with veterans who served in troubled times that remain clear as yesterday. They will be "the boys" forever.

I always think it is touching when a woman says her husband is her best friend. But really now, he's her husband, he took a vow to be her support through thick and thin. Sure he had a choice, but he also has an obligation. A true friend just comes along and supports without any need to vow eternal allegiance. There are many times women in particular will bare their souls to friends more openly than they will to spouses. Friends know how to keep confidences, offer suggestions. Friends know when you need a hug, and sometimes when you need a push too. I'm sure there are spouses who can accomplish all this in fine fashion, and they must be saints!

Friends can come into our lives in the most interesting ways, often by sheer coincidence. A complete stranger stopped me in a fabric store once to see if I could recommend a dressmaker. She needed ME, of course. That lucky encounter led to a friendship that endures to this day. We go months without visiting, until often on the same day we will call each other. We share our photos and our families, catch up on each other's lives, and perhaps won't see each other again for a long time. In fact, I'll call Ann right this minute. (She's fine, and was on her way to call me. Isn't that amazing?)

I'd say we're doing pretty well if we can count our true friends on ten fingers. There were four of us in Dartmouth when our children were little, and we still share a bond established while tying little hockey skates and doing craft projects. It was a special time for us young married moms with little money but plenty of drive and a desire to lay down friendship roots to last forever, since we all knew we would move along to other places in time. Although Laurie still lives there, and Karen is in Bridgewater, Dianne is way out in Condor, Alberta, and I'm in the middle. We had a coffee party a couple of years ago. On the first Monday morning in April at the stroke of the time signal on CBC we all sat down and had coffee wherever we were and wrote a postcard to all the others. I could nearly feel the vibes across the country!

There are also my mom and my sister. My mom's gone now, although I often hear her voice when I need it, and my sister is as near as the phone. When friends come as family it is an extra blessing. I know there are dads and brothers who are just as dear.

Look around at the people you know. I hope you see a lot of friends, people who are genuinely interested in the answer to the big question: "How are you, anyway?" Some with whom you work might only want to know if you're coming in to spread your germs, or if you're going to spare them the anguish of seeing you unproductive. Some who are good acquaintances will likely be much more sincere, but won't want to hear all the gory details. It's probably best to just reply, "Not too bad", and move on. However, your true friends will not only listen to everything you need to say, but also will make you tea and commiserate with you. We all need these people in our lives.

Now, this friends business is two-sided. You reap what you sow. Celebrate and cherish the relationships that seem to fall from the sky when two people become well and truly all-time good companions. The strangest coincidences will result in these special bonds: a chance encounter on a volunteer job, both being left-handed, whatever. Some spark flies, and you know this is the start of a lasting friendship. Both of you will always know there is someone out there who really cares what you are feeling. Both of you can rest assured that the other will understand not only the crazy things, but also the serious things that keep our lives vibrant. In order to reach this happy state of affairs, you need to be willing to share a bit of yourself. Trust and respect your friendship and nurture it to keep it alive and well, and forever you will be comfortable in the knowledge that you are a special person to someone else. What more could we ask than some day to be introduced as, "This is my friend."

Oh dear, I hope I'm not going to be eating shoe leather over this one! However, I'm sure there are countless grandmothers who will identify with my message. It's a good thing we were perfect parents when our kids were young.

I'M COUNTING TO TEN

I'm hauling old Nellie out of the barn. The last time I did this she got into a lather, all splay-legged and wild-eyed. Well, giddy-up old girl; I'm on my high horse again.

When did we stop raising our kids and start this business of "parenting"? I'm hearing a lot of "parenting" palaver lately, which I guess isn't surprising considering the age of the generation producing progeny these days. There's been a change in focus, from the children, as in "raising the kids", to the adults, as in "parenting".

Stand back as a "parented" two-year old throws himself into a perfect little fit. Watch the action, secure in the knowledge that "we wouldn't put up with that for one second!" First the child is treated to how his behavior is affecting his mother's anger management mechanisms, detailed in calm tones barely audible above the screaming. Then we hear a heart-to-heart discussion delivered at the child's level (that would be on bended knee!) on why this behavior is unacceptable. Finally, as a last resort Mom starts the ten-count routine. By this point, either the child is worn out from the tantrum, referred to as a melt-down, or Mom is conceding, or Grandma has headed for the wine cupboard and doesn't hear the grand finale.

An incident that should have lasted ten seconds has escalated into a full-blown behavioral problem. The child is dragged off to the psychologist and therapist who thrive on all this intense interaction. They are allowing the children to control the show in the name of supporting parents who have read one article too many about child-rearing instead of trusting their instincts and just doing the job. I have a friend who says the secret to child rearing is to get up early, and just keep walking till 7 p.m. Then it's bedtime for the little ones and you can rest up to start again the next morning. She has three well-adjusted kids, who know when Mom speaks, she means business. She's there for them every minute of the day, playing, wiping runny noses, reading to them, and yes, delivering a swift smack or little kisses, whatever is needed.

Here's one for you: I heard a mother say her child has "been gifted with learning disabilities." Don't you think that kid must really look forward to Christmas, knowing his learning problems are "gifts"? Call it like it is, Mom, your son has problems that are in no way gifts. He's special, sure, but he needs serious help, not mollycoddling over semantics. If you can't help him yourself, get him a tutor, but don't let him get away with thinking he is "gifted". Further, don't let him use those disabilities as a crutch for lack of effort.

There's something else. Children are wrapped in security from the moment they are shackled in the first baby car seat. They see the world as a danger zone a mine-sweeper couldn't navigate. At Chapters one Saturday an earnest dad was having his two little girls examine the ceiling to see the good lighting and, by the way, the sprinkler system. "We don't need a shower, Daddy", said Miss Curly-top. "Oh, no," says Dad, "but when [not if, but when!] a fire breaks out they will come on." And then he proceeded to tell them how we would all get out safely. He did this loud enough that everyone enjoying a Saturday sip at Starbucks was ready to head for the door. Can't kids enjoy an outing without everything becoming an educational activity?

There are shelves of magazines devoted to doing the right thing for your children, each one a cornucopia of advertising for toys, educational aids, and summer camps. What an industry this child bearing has spawned! All for the sake of little mites that want nothing more than a mommy and daddy to love them and treat them with respect. They haven't asked to participate in the baby battle to see which child has the biggest advantage at the earliest age. They don't care if they are sleeping in a $200.00 stroller or the old hand-me-down, as long as there is a reliable driver behind the handle.

When we were raising our kids - you knew I was getting to this - we listened to our hearts, our mothers, our neighbours, or the good old VON nurse, and did what we felt was best within our abilities. Our kids learned at an early age to steer a straight course and stay out of trouble, since Mom's patience didn't run to describing every nuance of emotion while she was heading for the wooden spoon. We were fair and firm. We gave them lots of time, since we were stay-at- home moms in most cases.

There are still some old-fashioned parents around, and oh my, their children are a joy! In fact, those are the kids who seem the most well-adjusted of all. The melt-down is not in their bag of tricks, nor is spending time in the bookstore checking out the fire alarm system. Their behavior and education come as a result of active living that includes taking calculated risks, and I can tell you, there is no psychologist practicing who can dish out that kind of experience from a case study.

Parents need to dig themselves out from under the pile of magazines, and stop trying to be perfect. Kids don't want "perfect," they want "there". That is to say, they want parents to be present, to set rules and limits that they mean to enforce. Kids don't need choices for everything from their breakfast to their bedtime; just tell them how it's going to be, and save the aggravation and arguing. Take the opportunity to be in control of everything while you can, I say! Give kids experience and let them learn as they go, don't force every new baby fad down their tiny throats - sign language at 6 months, swimming lessons at 9 months, and on it goes. They'll grow up a lot happier and likely not as frazzled. For sure, the parents will be less hysterical. "Because I say so", could become your mantra!

Oh, oh, old Nellie's tongue is hanging out. Best we head on back, and I ease myself out of the high horse saddle. Yikes, I'm gittin' a mite stiff in my old age. Crotchety too!

WHY I'M GLAD I'M NOT FIFTEEN

I really think being fifteen would be the worst age. "You're too young to do THAT!" "You're too old to act like THIS!" "Grow up, why don't you?" "My little girl." Yikes, how is a kid to know? Like, I mean, you'd think parents and teachers could see that a fifteen-year-old should be allowed, like, a whole pile of freedom, right?

I couldn't be fifteen. I'd never fit into those skin-tight bell-bottomed pants that drag at the heels, and my stomach would freeze, exposed under the skimpy T-shirt. I couldn't scrunch my shoulders trying to look cool when what I really would be is seriously cold. The platform soles on the winter boots could hardly be called practical, even though they'd give me a couple of inches of stature. Sitting on the Hub steps in January isn't my idea of cozy, but it is the place to see and be seen, and at fifteen it beats watching TV with your family or doing homework.

I could start a big harangue on how when I was a teenager in a small town we weren't even allowed to wear pants to school, we couldn't be out past nine on a school night, and our idea of big entertainment was a basketball game in the school gym. We led a sheltered existence, no doubt there, and we didn't even know we were hard done by!

We dressed funny; at least our parents thought so. We had hairstyles that defied gravity thanks to the wonders of hairspray. And don't get me started on the music. Rock and Roll was sweeter than the stuff our parents liked, could be loud and raucous, and lead to crazy dancing. Decadent beyond!!

It won't come as a surprise that our parents were as old-fashioned as they come, and equally stodgy as parents today. They thought fifteen year olds must have sprung from some alien planet, just as we thought they must have dropped from a time warp. They could think up house rules to ruin every fun thing we wanted to do; they led us to believe we were the source of every gray hair they had. Sound familiar?

Even if I could squeeze myself into the clothes, I would have a great deal of trouble squeezing into the mindset of a present day fifteen year old.

I really wonder how they cope as well as they do. They are bombarded with choices we never had to make. Their education demands that they make career path decisions when in fact they haven't lived long enough to truly know where their future will send them. And what an array of careers they might choose! Should they be engineers or entomologists; should they be musicians or meat cutters? And how will they afford this education when the time comes? These are no small worries as they try to stay on top of a new curriculum, often bereft of the basic necessities to learning.

Oh, sure, the Internet beckons. A wealth of information or an overload? Where our knowledge came from the books in the school library, the text-books, or what we could glean from radio and TV, teenagers now have too much to assimilate, pass judgment on, and store for future use. Is it any wonder the temptation exists to "sneak a smoke behind the shed", and check out some of the trash floating in cyberspace? Is it any wonder the time crunch lures them to plagiarism?

And who's around to monitor what fifteen year olds are finding? Who has the time? The demon word "BUSY" often leaves young people to the mercy of peer pressure, a powerful force too late thwarted. "Mom says I can't" got us over a lot of rough places years ago. Sometimes we even used it as our own excuse when we needed someone else to take the blame for us. Rules were set out not only by parents, but also by teachers, Girl Guides and Boy Scouts, Sunday school, whatever. The Ten Commandments expanded to about two hundred if we counted every one! Teenagers must find it hard now to condense the morals of the media, video games, even sports into a code of ethics by which they can conduct themselves. The very forces against which we railed were actually a comfort to us; they gave us a sense of security. We knew if we did as we were told life would be a lot simpler, that's for sure. (That's not to say we didn't stretch it to the limits sometimes. Oh, yes, parents knew all too well what grounding meant - except we weren't even allowed the telephone!)

We conceive of our young people as more mature that we were at their age. We think of them as confident, intelligent beyond their years. We think we really don't understand them, since their technological savvy and skills have surpassed us. But that's not true at all. In reality, they are no different than we were at fifteen. They need our advice, they want rules, they crave our attention, even if they stomp their feet and declare they don't.

We do our young people a disservice if we dismiss them out of hand. They are trying so hard to grow up responsibly and it's not always easy. When we can get past our own distrust of their dress and, yes, occasionally language, we will find fifteen-year-olds deserve our respect for their ingenuity, their knowledge, and their strength of character they are busy building on their own. All we have to do is talk to them - not nag, but talk! Maybe being fifteen wouldn't be so bad after all. Let's see, I could dye my hair purple, and get a Web page of my own, and….

This piece came after a summer of watching children test their wings in many pursuits. They grow so fast over a summer; activities they couldn't accomplish in June are easy by August. We watch in trepidation, but applaud their successes. It makes parenting hard at times.

"...SO THIS WON'T EVER HAPPEN AGAIN."

Try it. Take a chance. Give it a go. Risk, even on a small scale, is good for us. It gives us an adrenaline rush, it makes us know we are alive. It allows us to learn our boundaries; it delineates the "stupid line", as Alison called it. That's the line you mustn't cross, no matter how risky an activity is.

Children need risk in their lives. That's why we have playgrounds, for heavens sake! Kids need to climb monkey bars and hang upside down. They need to perch on the top of the big kids' slide and whiz down. They need to cling to the ropes of the swing while Dad gives them a big push-through. It doesn't hurt that their little stomachs might be given a turn with all the excitement; what's important is that they tried, they conquered a fear, they moved up to "big kids stuff".

Now, this is when the game gets serious. When babies learn to walk, they walk away. It's really hard to watch this happen, and we always want to grab those little hands so they don't fall. Actually, what we should do is stand by, guide little steps with a hand behind to catch the fall, not prevent it. How does a little person learn when he has gone too far otherwise?

Steps lead to wheels, and now the risk is multiplied. Little trikes can teach children about falling off, about going too fast, about smashing into things, about how cross Mom was when you rode over the flower bed! If the child is allowed to learn these things on his own, the lessons will sink in well.

Move on to this summer of wheels, when it was difficult to negotiate the sidewalks without encountering a skateboarder (whom I really secretly revere!), a scooter or a bicycle, rocketing past. I resorted to "old lady ranter" one afternoon and admonished a young man to "get that thing on the road where it belongs". All I needed were the black oxfords and the apron and I'd have looked like my Grandma! These kids were engaging in what to them seemed innocuous fun, but to me it was unnecessary risk.

After that encounter I started to notice risky bike behaviour. Bad enough to be watching for deer on a dark night, we were met head on by cyclists with no lights, tearing down the wrong side of the road. Two young lads must have thought helmets would save their lives and shiny new trick bikes when they shot out in front of my car at an intersection. I stopped to let them know how frightened I'd been by their thoughtless behaviour. Their mother was very apologetic. Their degree of risk was definitely over the stupid line. I don't think they'll do that again, in particular after Mom got finished the tongue-lashing.

We try to make all summer activities safe but, by taking away all the risk, we are giving our children a false sense of security. They can't play near water (they might drown); they can't go gallivanting off through the forest (the bears are around); they can't use the playground (the equipment is dangerous). However, if we were to let them try on a limited scale, widening their experience as they were able to handle the situation, I believe we would be raising responsible children who would understand their limits without our having to continually set them. Yes, bad things happen. Yes, we all have to be careful. But no, emphatically, we do not have to give up the things we enjoy because of one bad experience.

Every time we hear of these awful accidents that lead to tragedies beyond comprehension, our law-makers are quick to instigate all sorts of restrictions so "this will never happen again". Well, it WILL happen again. People will succumb to boating accidents, fires, mountain climbing, and other activities in which they were taking a risk, testing their limits. However, they must take responsibility for their own actions to whatever degree they can, and that is only possible if they have learned through experience what their personal boundaries of safety entail. No governing body can set the limits arbitrarily.

Our kids were cyclists, road racers to be exact. If you don't think that is a scary activity to watch, stand by a pack of cyclists bearing down on a leader coming around a corner, wheels screaming. The only scarier thing is seeing your daughter in the lead and her wheel skidding out from under her as three other cyclists careen right over her and her bike. She finished the race; it nearly finished me!! She knew the risk, prepared for the fall, and overcame it. I, on the other hand, nearly had a heart attack!

Our responsibility to our young people is to help them set their limits, always mindful that they will go one step farther to see if we are right. They are going to graduate to more and more powerful wheels, more and more dangerous activities, all in the urge to reach their maximum adrenaline rush. We want to prepare them for the excitement without restricting them so much that the activity is cushioned beyond enjoyment. We can't get caught up in fear to the point that our kids' only rush comes from living vicariously through video games.

Let them climb the monkey bars; the next climb could be to the Everest Base Camp. Let them fly down the slide; the next slide could be the Olympic ski hill. Just stand behind with a parent's hand at their back to catch them if they do fall. Don't let them see you fussing over every scratch or gulp of lake water swallowed. Don't continually admonish them, but let them experience life in an effort to discover for themselves the limits of their own abilities. Guide them to make the right decisions and trust them not to cross that "stupid line". Caution yes, of course. Cushioning, maybe. Cocooning, no.

Never let it be said that small towns have no action. We keep so busy we can't even think about going on a holiday over the summer, since we might miss something fun. Not only do we like to attend everything, we like to be on the helping end, too. That's where our friends are, after all.

I'M "FESTED" OUT!

One summer when we were very young, we had a distant cousin come for a visit. He was a pudgy kid, I remember, whiny and snotty-nosed. He'd sit in the middle of the kitchen and carp at his mother, "Ada, I got nuthin' to do!"

Ada was not much help here, and instead of letting Bertram (honestly, that was his name!) enjoy some idle time until he found something on his own, she entertained him endlessly. Mother rolled her eyes, sniffed a note of disgust, and did her best to ignore him. Sue and I were never caught in this situation since we had imaginations that took us happily from breakfast to bedtime. Idleness was definitely not part of our vocabulary. Eventually Bertam's mantra became part of our family lore, but only as a joke.

If Bertram were living in this area, he never would be able to claim "nuthin'" to do. On the contrary, there is so much going on, we can't keep up with it. In June the summer stretched like a soft ribbon to fall, but that was not to be. We rushed headlong from the Riveredge Artsfest to the Puppets Up festival, with all the "fests" in between: Celtfest, Gospelfest, Herbfest, and Bloomfest.

All this activity has made me think I should host a few "fests" of my own. The first will be "Jamfest," but it might be cancelled if the temperature falls below 30. The event starts about 8 a.m. when everyone heads out to pick berries. Find your goofiest hat and some T-shirt with a message. ("My wife is the berries!") Don't worry about the sun or the bugs. What's summer without them, ha ha? Sweat beads on your forehead are the fashion statement, so ignore them. Be sure to take little ones on these outings, as they are great little pickers who rarely get sick from eating too many berries. Now, home for the real fun part of the day. Get out those jars, get the water boiling, and get those berries cleaned. (Making lunch on the side is good for extra points here!) You can do the berry dance over the dog who is gobbling up the ones you drop, and look forward to washing that floor as a reward for the great pile of jam you're making. This "fest" calls out for shortcake, so it's best to have the oven on all day too. The big prize will be at least two pounds sweated off by dinner time, and just enough time left to plan how you're going to deal with the dog who's sick from eating berries. A fun-filled day can be had by all!

Join us in early August for Weedfest. We'll have a gay old time, each taking a bed to clean up. We'll make jolly piles of that awful grass stuff that's invaded everything. We'll have competitive dead-heading contests where everyone gets a chance to snap heads off the sulking annuals. While the moms try to wrestle the tomato vines into a semblance of order, the dads will be having fun changing the cords on the Weed Whackers. Kids can try their luck scooping angel hair algae out of the pond without falling in. Good thing we only celebrate this event once a year!

The following week will be "Zucchinifest." Here's your opportunity to taste this not-so-rare summer treat that every good cook has to hide in a recipe - muffins, cakes, casseroles, milkshakes, whatever. Be sure to enter your recipe early, as there will be a pile of them to sample. The only caveat is you have to use MY zucchini! There'll be activities for the whole family. Enter the zucchini baseball tournament; try your hand at the cabre toss with the ones that lurk under the leaves until they are gargantuan. The kids and grandparents will love the country zucchini drop! Who can leave the most zucchinis on their neighbour's porch without getting caught? You can also adopt-a-zucchini to have enough seeds to start your own patch. (We might let only city folk in on this action; they still think zucchini come in neat little supermarket packages.) After the festivities, we'll invite the neighbour's chickens over to clean up the dross, as they are the only animals I have ever seen attack those babies with gusto.

For the last week in August, we're planning "Restfest". Ahhh, the best till the last! That's the week we're going to gather all the volunteers who have worked on the other "fests" to sit back and relax. The most energetic activities for the week will be slicing sweet slabs of watermelon and moving the chairs to a cooler corner. Meals will be minimal, with some combination of tomatoes, peppers, and onions. You're welcome to join in, no charge, but don't be looking for games and prizes. However, we would make you really welcome if you brought cold liquid refreshment of the brown variety, if you get my drift. For entertainment, we'll trade "what I did this summer" stories, and we'll get the kids hyped for September. But wait, don't go there yet: that's for next month when we have "Back-to-school fest".

No doubt about it, Bertram, you'd be a busy boy if you lived here. The talent, innovation, and energy required to drive these summer festivals comes from the love of our area. Every person who has contributed valuable summer hours to make them a success deserves a free pass to our "Restfest". Thank you, thank you, from all of us who enjoyed the music, the flowers, the food, and the fun you provided. You are indeed special people!

This may upset your calendar, but once you've heard me out, I think you will agree that the first of January, the middle of winter, is not the best time to instigate big changes. We are too busy trying to stay warm to think about starting something momentous and new. The first day of school begins the New Year as surely as Labour Day tolls the end of summer. Be brave, strike out on a new path!

HAPPY NEW YEAR

New Year falls on September 3 this year. According to the our home-grown philosophy, we are entitled to claim September as a great celebration month: neither in one year nor in another, on the cusp of change in all aspects of activities, ready to embrace a new season, the chance to explore prospects and perhaps set our lives in a new direction.

We felt the change in the air as soon as the Back to School flyers hit the house. On a trip through Wal-Mart, tanned and tattered little boys looked for a new game to satisfy the ennui of late summer, while sisters were eyeing the new school supplies. Poor Mom was caught in the middle: new shoes or new jeans, neither looking too exciting. The countdown is on till the first day of school. Even a weekend at the cottage has lost its appeal - books all dog-eared, bathing suits limp on the porch rail, summer projects abandoned on the beach. The school buses are being washed and fueled, drivers are being trained, and a few parents are looking forward to that yellow convoy rolling down the country roads.

For many young people, this is the start of independence: college, university, or a new job. They spread their wings and fly away as surely as those little swallows on the power lines fly off. They will come home again, but they will never be little kids again. Can you deny parents a tear and a Kleenex when they see their offspring wave good-bye from a dorm residence? No more than the young mom watching her four-year old trundling through the kindergarten doors for the first time. Once children learn to walk, they walk away, just as it should be too.

So how will we start the New Year? We are considering our options. This is the ideal time for a New Year's resolution to strengthen the physique, the spirit or mind: art classes, exercise programmes all beckon. Once you've signed up and paid your money, you are much more likely to see the project through than if you strike out on your own. That notion led us to pottery classes, a trip to France, dog agility classes, and more, all of which we thoroughly enjoyed. Retirement can keep a person busier than work, for goodness sake.

I think the whole garden needs a fresh start too, so it will get dug over and replanted next week. It's looking tired and no amount of watering can make up for summer drought. No cucumbers ripening, no pumpkins coming along, no second crop of radishes. But no lack of zucchinis!! Does nothing deter that plant?!?

So where will we start on the New Year Celebration? On Labour Day we'll have a wonderful summer picnic with potato salad, corn on the cob, and blueberry pie. We'll get out the summer photos, relive the best moments, laugh over the silly ones, and keep out two or three to frame. We'll fill our garden journal with a summary of our crops or lack thereof, and note how the sun is setting earlier now. And then we'll get out the course calendars and choose one each, just something to fill our all too few spare hours.

A note of caution: in your zeal to re-invent yourself, in the effort to fill the gap when your house is empty of young people's laughter and music, in your exuberance over the wealth of new activities, make time to relax and smell the last roses of summer. Add up your activities - and your children's too - and don't have to be somewhere every day. Also, make a resolution to avoid the expression, "I'm too busy. I haven't got time." That's all we have - use it wisely. Leave time to meditate, to have tea with a friend, to love one another just a little more than last year.

Raise your glasses to the New Year, and the best to all of you!

School days, school days! They sure aren't like when we were young. But wait, they really are: the same apprehension, the same stress. We just didn't call it stress, we called it working hard and seeing results. It's a hard lesson, but we all have to learn it, parents, teachers, and most of all kids.

ADVICE FOR THE SCHOOL-BOUND

Last week, my little next-door neighbour and I were discussing going back to school. "Don't say the 's' word when Mom's around," she whispered. "It makes her sad." She was right about that too. In early May the family starts counting down the remaining school days, and their summer is full of happy times. There is nothing gives us greater pleasure than hearing those four little kids playing all summer, and Mom and Dad enjoying it too. They all are sorry to see school start again, not the usual thing you hear parents say as August winds down, and kids are bored with everything.

Returning to school filled me with trepidation when I was young. However, I think that was a good thing; made me realize the importance of the whole process, and instilled some pressure to succeed. We always started school with new clothes, new shoes that usually pinched and blistered, and all new supplies. That part I loved. Here's a little aside: we lived in Trail, B.C., a company town where everyone's father worked for Cominco. It was only when I started university that I realized pencils came from a store, and that not all pencils had "Safety is your business, safety is our business" along the edge! Everyone in Trail had company pencils the fathers brought home from work. Cominco's legacy to literacy!

I watch kids returning to school now, and often think what a long road they have ahead of them, even the nonchalant teenagers pushing and shoving their way off the school bus. They may not realize it now, but the time they spend in school shapes the rest of their lives. They need to make the most of it, not waste their opportunities, not expect that they can achieve without some effort, and not take their precious education for granted.

There are ways to achieve this lofty ideal. However, it takes students, parents, and teachers working together. It's not just the school that bears the brunt of the education process. So here's my advice, for what it's worth.

To students I would say, school work presents a huge challenge. Sometimes you might find yourself at crossroads where it is easy to go astray. You march along an unfamiliar path until you are so hopelessly lost you give up the whole trip. Not a good plan. As soon as you think you are heading off the path, ask for help. Ask a teacher, ask a parent, ask someone you trust. You have to speak up for yourself, or no one will know you are falling behind. School is a hard place, but everyone wants you to succeed. Don't be distracted by what your classmates are doing. Your task is to do the very best you can do. It's like a job you go to every day, and your pay is the knowledge you are gaining.

Respect your teacher as a person and as a source of knowledge. Every once in a while, thank your teacher for something he has done for you, even if it's just being there every day. Same goes for your parents!

Sacrifice your game-boy time and your TV time to reading something you like. I don't care if it's magazines or novels, just so long as you read every day. Pretty soon it will become a good habit. (Sure, read in bed with a flashlight if you like. We all have done that and it's fun.)

Fill your leisure time with pursuits that build your self-esteem and your body. Find a sport you like, and do it with enthusiasm. Play hockey, even if you're not very good. Be part of a team where you have a common bond with friends. Find a school activity you really enjoy: radio club, drama, chess. You'll see your teachers in a new light, and learn many new things. Just don't fritter your life away with no purpose or plan. Take responsibility for yourself in everything you do. Even if you're only six, you can do this. Ask for help when you need it; do it yourself when you can.

Spend time with your family. Parents can be really cool people if you give them a chance. Who knows, they might even be able to teach you a thing or two! Include them in your activities, as they enjoy seeing you grow with your peers. They were young once, and know what you're going through. Make your parents proud by sharing yourself with them. They love you, after all.

Now parents, you are walking a narrow trail on this journey. You walk behind with your hand out to catch a fall or to give a little push. The difficulty arises in knowing when to do what! From the time little ones board their first school bus, they are learning to cope alone, but it reassures them to know that somewhere back there is a caring parent. So do just that: CARE. Care enough to listen not only to what they tell you, but also to what they imply. Care enough to help with school work without doing the projects; you are past getting marks for your poster work! Care enough to intercede on their behalf when they encounter difficulties. Care enough to talk to your kids, and I mean really talk. Fill them in on your thoughts, your feelings, not just your "orders," and maybe they will be more open to sharing theirs.

Give your children opportunities outside school to develop their many talents. It will improve their school work. Take your kids, don't send them. Learn what you can about their chosen pursuits. However, don't put on added pressure by demanding perfection. We have all seen the horror of parents living vicariously through their offspring. Above all, be proud of your children in whatever they do. Don't con them with false praise, but do congratulate their triumphs, even when they are small. Love them dearly; they grow up too fast, and they need to know always that you are on their side.

Teachers are the third part of this equation, and a major one. On you falls the huge task of imparting a vast amount of prescribed knowledge to many in a short time. You are expected to lead the way, chase down the ones who veer off the path, prod the stragglers, even provide maps for those who run on ahead. This assignment demands that you take their needs into consideration before your own. You are teaching children, not a subject. They will learn English or Math - or not- in spite of your efforts, but they will not learn how to grow as people without your help. When you stand at the front of the room, they are looking to you to awaken their desire to learn. No amount of academia will make up for lack of enthusiasm. However, a genuine interest in your subject matter will quickly transfer to your students.

Put the kids who need the most help in the front row, where you can talk directly to them. Put the trouble-makers along one side where you can keep an eye on them. Include them all in your discussions. If you see they are not concentrating, they may be encountering difficulties. Stop right there and rescue them. Don't wait for exam time to see they are failing. It's easy to teach to the smartest students, but they can usually manage on their own.

Be honest with your students. Mark them fairly and constructively. Give them the opportunity to improve on their efforts, and when they do extra work, give them credit for it. Help them to improve by example, not criticism. If they need outside help, work with their tutor or parent to maximize the time for which they are paying. A tutor isn't a threat to you, he is an adjunct who can make your record look good too!

Treat your students and their parents with respect. Don't wait for an interview if you suspect a problem. Talk to the parents on a personal basis as a member of the learning team, not as the figure of authority. A quiet talk over a coffee is more beneficial than the interview where the parent sits in the little chair and the teacher is at the big desk!

So there we have it, a trek on the highway to learning that might make this school year a little easier for all concerned. The year always starts with good intentions, and perhaps if everyone really talks to each other when the going gets tough, really listens when problems surface, and really takes the time to care, then school can be a pleasure instead of a chore for so many students.

Good luck to every shiny faced student, either six or sixteen. I hope your school year will be a joy to you. Just remember, everyone is there to help you succeed.

Spring cleaning is a dangerous time when I decide to get rid of excess. Stand back when I start pitching stuff, as I've been known to be too zealous and have thrown away things I should have kept. Then I have to go "garbage diving", not my favourite pastime.

"GETTING AND SPENDING…"

There's a poetry line somewhere that says something like, "The world is too much with us; late and soon, getting and spending, we lay waste our powers." I'm a great proponent of that philosophy. We all have 'way too much "stuff." And possessing all this "stuff" puts a large burden on our lives.

I'm not an avid shopper. I much prefer to get it and get out, so to speak. Wandering aisles leaves me not only exhausted but a little disgusted. The women's wear section of any department store is a good example: racks and racks of clothes, every size, colour, and style. While women paw through the selection, whining about never finding the right stuff, there are thousands of items that will be on sale racks, discard piles, and ultimately recycled in the not too distant future.

So what if these items were taken home? They would be stored in closets packed with other clothes, most only worn once or twice. In the meantime, the owner has to find hangers, keep them all sorted, feel guilt when they were expensive and not worn enough, store them when the season is over, or pack them off to the Hub, where once again they will be sorted, stored…. You get the picture.

We all possess too many "things", and these "things" take a toll on our personal resources. If a person collects anything of value, he is expected to display his collection, clean it, insure it, and worry so much he might even go to the extreme of installing an alarm system to foil intruders. Further, he is hounded by the desire to possess more items for his collection, making him prey for sellers. When all is said and done, what becomes of his collection? It likely is auctioned for mere cash, not loved for the intrinsic joy of possessing for which it was originally purchased.

Downsizing can be an eye-popping experience, especially if one has lived in the same house for a few decades. What to take, what to leave, what to pitch? Every item seems to conjure up memories, some too poignant to discard. But consider, the memories will last forever and take up no space, while "stuff" deteriorates, crowds the dickens out of living quarters, and consumes our energies. We can retrieve memories clear as day whenever we like without having to sort, store, clean or accumulate. What a blessing!

How cathartic it is to clean out our "stuff", and dispose of it! Let someone else have the joy of it for a while and then dispense with it too. When my dear mother died, we were amazed at her collection of odd little knickknacks. Some we remembered and I have to admit I did squirrel a few of those away, but in general they were her treasures, not ours, and we let them go. I'm sure some are gracing shelves to this day, treasures once again, but not in my house.

Alan will tell you I'm downright dangerous when I go on a cleanout rampage. He practically has to hide his stuff or I'd have it out to the trash in an instant. My zeal has been harmful more than once when I've thrown out cheques and valuable papers, but I have a need to extract myself from the weight of too many things. I sometimes feel as if I'm buried in belongings when I'm searching in vain for a lost item, when in the depths of a closet I discover a sweater I've completely forgotten , when I have more pictures than wall space on which to hang them. At that point, I go into overdrive, and the Hub becomes the recipient of a LOT of "stuff."

Oh, how much better I feel when I can see the countertops again, when there is an empty drawer, when there are only a few pairs of shoes and not ten in the cupboard! I need to do this on a regular basis to unclutter my life. Obviously lots of others feel the same way, as that is the backbone of our wonderful Hub store.

When summer comes, we can enjoy the open spaces for a few months. But wait, do I see a little spot in the garden where I can put another plant? Excuse me a moment here, I'm just going to run down to the nursery and see if I can buy some green thing to stick in there. Oh, come on, plants aren't "stuff", are they?

When fall beckons and you know you will be inside for months, you begin to feel the confines need revamping. That's the diplomatic way of saying the whole place needs a face-lift! Yikes, there is nothing more dangerous that a woman with paint chips in her pocket!

BITTEN, SMITTEN, AND PAINT-SPLATTERED

It's a sunny day with trees splashed a kaleidoscope of colour. Frost is glittering on the roof, fog is lifting off the neighbour's pond, and I want to capture it all to last right through to next March. I wander in the woods picking up leaves, which I can lay out in a fan like a paint palette.

Oh, there now, I've said it! Last week I was meandering down the street when the siren song of the decorating shop beckoned. As if in a trance, I was lured past the fabric samples, all of which I have to touch - very bad sign. And then I was standing in front of my real nemesis: the paint samples!! So there I was, taking those compelling little strips one at a time, pondering greys or yellows. The shop owner knows my weakness, and offered me the rainbow in the form of the whole catalogue of paint strips, not only to browse, but to take home!!

It only gets worse. Now I have it splayed out, and have the choice narrowed to two tones of yellow. I can see what's coming next: I'm convincing myself this will be a small task, only one room after all. Likely only take me a day, two at most. The furniture will have to be moved out, but that's not a bad thing. Yes, two days and we'll have a totally new look.

The last time I did this, I went through this very same routine. I approached the project sort of sideways. I cleaned out dresser drawers first, cleaned out the closet too. I cleared everything off the flat surfaces, and polished the dresser tops. That was Day 1. Day 2, I took down the curtains and washed the windows. Note that as yet I haven't mentioned painting. I was hoping a thorough cleaning would satisfy my urge to re-decorate, but I didn't put the curtains back. Day 3, I decided I'd rearrange all the paintings. And therein lay my undoing. None of them matched the room colour as it was. I never should have done that.

Now that I had the room pulled apart, I had the preparation underway - practically finished, I thought. (Am I not a master of persuasion?) Might as well bite the bullet and buy new paint. I get so excited choosing a colour, seeing it mixed, getting my pristine paint brush and rollers, those neat little stir sticks. It all looks so tidy and easy. The paint practically puts itself on the walls.

Such a project is more fun if shared, don't you think? If I was going to paint, it should be a "we" project, not what my dear husband had planned for his morning. We dragged furniture out of the room, got out the plastic drop sheets, and devised a gate to keep doggy paws out of the way. We were into the big stuff now, no turning back.

Day 1 of the job involved Alan on a ladder with a roller doing the ceiling that I can't do and that he dislikes. Happy moment there! I did the claustrophobic closets that left me sporting attractive green streaks in my hair. Miles of paint tape covered every straight edge to ensure a fast application of trim paint, but I hadn't accounted for the fiddly bits around the window frames. Good thing the paint is water washable.

Day 2 and we were still speaking, although Alan opined that the job was bigger than I'd led him to believe. (I may go into politics!) A morning saw the first coat of dark green on the walls. Hmmm, a little darker than I'd thought it would be, but maybe when it dried… At this point, Alan thought it best to step back from the project while I let my imagination run rampant. He was afraid I wanted to start all over again.

What started as a small project was escalating, with little splatters of green migrating to the carpet, my hair, of course my clothes, and even the poor dog. But no matter, I soldiered on. Day 3, and by now meals were deteriorating to cans of this and that while I got on with the painting. In a desperate effort to get life back to normal, Alan offered to help again, but I was over the edge. I had decided that a "faux finish" would soften the green and highlight the curtain colour. Back to the paint store for the exact right shade of paint, glaze, and other stuff to add a certain "je ne sais quoi" to my work.

Day 4 saw a lot of mixing, soft rags, exasperation, hungry husband, disgusted dog, and more paint splatters. I began to think this project would never end. But then I stood back and voila! It was exactly what I wanted. Success was mine! Or at least I thought discretion might be the better part of valour and I should stop right now!

Day 5: Clean-up day! That was the straw that broke the poor old paint camel's back. All day, we rearranged stuff, hung pictures and curtains, dragged furniture back, cleaned brushes, dumped the encrusted trays and paint sticks. We were nearly too tired to enjoy the total effect.

Now, you ask, why would a sane person do that again? Sometimes the stars are aligned and fate just takes over. You see, last week one of the clues in my crossword puzzle was " what you wear to paint". "Happy smile" didn't fit, but "old jeans" did. Isn't that a sign? Wasn't my bringing the paint palette home a sign? Weren't all those lovely fall leaves a sign? Of course!

Hey, Alan, don't you think this Honeywind Yellow would be the perfect thing for our room? It'll only take a couple of mornings to do.

I can do it myself. It'll be easy.

There are times when I feel my old lady hat heavy on my head. Maybe this is one of those times, but if we lose these civilities, what will be next? White shoes after Labour Day?

"JUST DON'T CALL ME
LATE FOR DINNER…"

There's a new trend afoot to which I can't relate, and I'll bet I'm not alone. When we were at a meeting a while back, we were all asked to introduce ourselves. Nearly everyone who spoke up gave only a first name! "Hi, I'm Sally." "Hi, I'm Jake." "Hi, my name's Angela." I nudged Alan and whispered none too quietly, "Sally WHO??" Okay, it likely sounded strange when I said "Glenda JONES," as if Jones were some really unique last name, but honestly I felt like I was at a Something Anonymous meeting where I wasn't supposed to garner too much information about anyone.

Is this a trend to keep part of ourselves private? Or is it just too much effort to recite both first and last names? Perhaps some people have totally unique first names like Cher or Prince, which tells us everything we need to know about them. Maybe I should become part of that group since "Glenda" is so rare a name that I can't ever find personalized pencils or fridge magnets. But then, when I introduce myself with only my first name, people often hear "Brenda" or "Glenna." Here's the funny part: when I add on the "Jones", people comment on such a fine Welsh name! I guess I was just very astute in marrying a Jones.

Maybe there's another reason for using only first names. Heaven forbid this next excuse: perhaps some people realize how bad we all are at remembering names, so choose to give us only one to struggle over instead of the full nine yards! I think I'm up to the challenge, though, if given half a chance.

Frankly, I find the one-name habit like waiting for the second shoe to drop. Besides, it sounds overly familiar, as when the waiter sidles up to your table, kneels down and announces, "I'm Bruce and I'll be your waiter tonight." Lord, I always feel like he wants us to adopt him or something!! I want to say, "Well, Bruce, I couldn't adopt you without knowing your pedigree."

There are some definite drawbacks for future communication too. If I know only your first name, how can I call you to invite you to the labyrinth* party? If you're not in the phone book under "Sally," your chances of phone soliciting may be nil, but also your hope of a date may go by the board too. Then there's the question of family ties. Are you a well-known local family or have you breezed into town like Mary Poppins? No wait, she had a second name too!

It's bad enough that genealogical ties are increasingly difficult with women keeping maiden names, and whole families having a variety of last names, but when we don't choose to identify ourselves with our families, we are denying our acquaintances the opportunity to connect us with our community. Most last names have significance, especially in small towns. Perhaps you're a Brydges, or Gamble, or Madore. Right away we can connect. We know your uncle, your mom, your brother. Right away, we have something in common to talk about.

I think it is likely good manners to introduce ourselves with both first and last names. A corollary to this trend is children calling adults by their first names. I figure if I'm taller than the little people, they should call me Mrs. Jones. And I really appreciate it when they do too. It's all going back to that respect concept, which is, after all, the basis of good manners. But I'll leave that for another time.

There are many tactics for remembering names. Eye contact, repetition in the first few seconds, an interesting remark to hold the speaker's attention will frequently jog your memory to hold on to the person's name. I must admit, if I'm in a group and I have a notepad, I'll write the names down. Desperate times, desperate measures!

Next time you're glad-handing your way through a group, notice how many times you get only a first name, and use that as an excuse to discover a little more about the person. Name-tags are notorious for being first name only. It doesn't give us much to go on, and makes me think the person mustn't be proud of his family ties, or must think he is so important we will forever after associate that name with him alone. Isn't that an ego trip?

So next time you get the first name treatment, don't be shy about being nosy and asking about the last name too. It'll likely be a conversation starter, or at least an opportunity to connect a little closer with an individual. As for me, you can call me Glenda, or Mrs. Jones if you're a little person, just don't call me late for dinner!

A note about our labyrinth: We used the only flat corner of our garden to install a 20-foot diameter labyrinth. It's a grass path outlined in paving bricks. We started with an awful pile of bricks, lugged home in several truckloads from the garden supply. We didn't count the bricks we used, but we have - ahem - a few left over. It seems our math isn't what it was when we were in Grade 6, and we figured out the AREA instead of the CIRCUMFERENCE. We remembered Πr but used the wrong formula. It should have been 2Πr but we used Πr². We were so proud of ourselves for being able to do the math without calling Engineer Son, Steve. However, it's given us a good story and a good laugh. We'll find a use for the bricks, no doubt.

Should you want to come see the labyrinth - and the brick pile, just give us a call, and we'd be happy to show it off. We're even in the provincial labyrinth registry.

Since I wrote this, we have heard several more sentences that have given us joy. Every one has been a surprise of the best sort. My wish is that the sentences you hear will take you on a pleasant walk. Watch for the soft woodsy places, and walk carefully over the sharp rocks. I hope that all the turns you make will lead to wonderful places, a route less travelled, an adventure that will enchant and enrich.

SENTENCES THAT CHANGE YOUR LIFE

Our woods are waiting for winter. The trails are crispy gold beech leaves, rustling with squirrels and the occasional grouse that Belle flushes out with such delight. We scuffle our way along the well-worn paths. Many happy hours have gone into moving the biggest rocks you can imagine to make the trail smooth and straight, cleaning the underbrush, chipping the old wood for soft walking. We know every tree, every big rock, every little turn so well that we can walk there in the night and not get lost. We love our woods.

Each of the nine paths has its unique features: flowers, lichens, a harp-shaped beech. We even have a few reminders of when the kids have come to visit: a chair we found way in the back, a little star Alison gave us one Christmas, a funny metal thing we think is…well, you'd have to see it! Our family feels close to us out in the woods, so we've named each trail for one of them. That way, even though they aren't here exactly, we feel their connection.

When we walk the trails, we usually go in one direction, but occasionally something will occur that changes our course completely. We might see a new tree down, or Belle might be too interested in a hole she's found, and we go off on a new tangent. We've discovered hepatica, tiny ferns, blueberry bushes, and gorgeous mushrooms, all because we got off the regular route. More than once we've incorporated those special places into a new path.

Now, I think life is sort of like that. We go along our merry way, one day following on the heels of the next when, out of the blue, one thing is said that makes us turn a big right angle. Life is never the same after that. There are the really big sentences: the "will you marry me" or the "I do" or the "I got a raise." They're monumentally important, no doubt. However, we all hope to hear those sentences and know what we expect to happen next. We can see the path ahead between the trees, and taking the hand of someone we love we set out together with little trepidation.

There are other sentences we never want to hear. We can all imagine them, fear them like the pox, and although we likely will hear them at some point in our lives, we don't let them into our minds too often. Indeed, they also change our lives, but the paths they make us tread can be very rocky and steep, and often we have to walk them alone, not happy trails for sure.

However, there are other little sentences we may not even register the first time we hear them, just little passing remarks can have a huge impact in the overall picture. In 1970 we were securely ensconced in Victoria with our two little boys and a comfortable home. I thought we'd be there forever, when Alan called to ask, "How would you like to move to Halifax?" Although moving across the country was the farthest thing from our minds, we set off on our big adventure. We packed up our stuff, sold the house, and four months later were enduring the dirty remains of a Halifax winter instead of gardening amongst the daffodils in Victoria. And what a wonderful time we had in Halifax, what cherished friends we made, what beautiful scenery we beheld! One sentence was all it took.

The second sentence I remember clearly was from David when he was about twelve: "I'd sure like to try those skates some time." Speed skates, he meant. And that led us into ten years of activities in which we'd never even had a passing interest. We got involved in a big way: Olympic organization, competitions, executive positions, fitness crazes, a whole raft of new friends, a sportswear business, and so much more. Alison followed Dave into the sport, with Steve becoming support crew. All of us became athletes. Why, I even ran two marathons thanks to the encouragement of the kids. Alan was a VIP at the Calgary Olympics, while I was an official who came home with the fancy jacket and all. When all was said and done, the change wrought by that one little sentence had huge impact, since both Dave and Alison went on to the University of Calgary to skate, and ultimately met their life loves there. Steve and I ran a successful small business for many years, all because Dave had a passion to try a new pair of skates!

One summer day in 1995 I casually mentioned, "I'd like to have a look at those Viceroy house models some time." Idle curiosity, even though we were in a house we liked in a good part of Ottawa. We stopped that very minute and walked into the house of our dreams. The affable salesman introduced us to his brother, the real estate agent in Almonte, and the rest is history, so to speak. We found our property a week later, and although it took us six months to actually own it, we knew it was meant to be and were willing to wait. Less than a year after we had set foot in that Viceroy house we were sitting in our living room overlooking our woods in awe of the corner we'd turned, thanks to one little sentence!

We're kept on our toes, wondering what the next sentence is going to be. However, we live by Alison's motto: "One just never knows; that's what makes life so exciting." We haven't had a sentence in a while, so we've been waiting for one. The mail has just been the "gimme" letters, the e-mail a storm of "forwards", nothing too exciting.

But last night the phone rang. Dave and Kim called from Calgary to see what our holiday plans are for next summer (next summer, for heaven's sake!) We've suggested we would go out and landscape for them, since their back yard needs real work. They think we should drive out and bring the dog so we can stay as long as we want…and here it comes!!!… "To visit your first grandchild!!!" So there you have it, another one of those great sentences that means life will never be the same again. We are getting new identities: Grandparents! We're off along another new section of life's pathway, a whole right angle turn from where we were not a minute before the phone rang. And we're very, very happy!

We have always had a boot closet that rivals a shoe store. When the kids were young it was runners, cycling shoes, skates, boots, ski boots, and more. You'd think the two of us would have a few less pairs, but somehow we have no fewer now. Besides, they all have to be out of sight of our little dog that punishes us by chewing the laces right back to the eyelets whenever he is annoyed. At least we can walk through the hall without tripping on assorted footwear.

FOOTLOOSE AND FANCY FREE

I love autumn. Although there is the anticipation of winter, the crisp leaves still lie fresh along our paths, the rain pools in the low places. There's only one way to enjoy being out in this weather, and that's to have the proper footwear. Cold wet feet do not make for pleasant outdoor times.

My life could be defined by my boot closet. Bring on winter: I'm ready! I am equipped for cold (good hiking boots), snow shovelling (very old Kodiaks), or working in the woods (my all time favourite work boots). I've also got the fancy and never warm dress boots that I rarely wear. Otherwise I make do with my running shoes, a cute euphemism as my running days are long behind me, thank heavens.

That was pretty well all until September when I became the caregiver for my neighbour's little menagerie. (An aside: I relish this task. The chickens, ducks and turkeys, cats and dogs give me no end of pleasure every day, and the eggs are wonderful. Alan is glad for me to do this, as it keeps me from wanting them all over here!) Every morning I was coming home with wet feet from slopping around with water buckets, cleaning pens, etc. (a lot of "etc."!). I finally indulged myself with the ultimate footwear: wonderful high black rubber boots. They were the least expensive addition to the closet, and absolutely the best purchase I have ever made. Excited? Definitely!

I know, you'd think after living in the country for a few years now, I'd have had these long ago. I can't explain it either, but now that I have them, I absolutely LOVE my boots. I can muck about in the barn, clean out the pond, walk in puddles, ignore the muddy road, and my feet stay warm and dry. I feel real "country" tromping about in my boots. In fact, I even wear them to town sometimes, especially if I'm in work mode. They are easy to get on and off, and sure do the trick in keeping pant cuffs clean. The only drawback is that as soon as the dogs see me reaching for the rubber boots, all notion of work has to be put on hold while we stride off through the woods for an extended walk.

Now, if we're heading off to do serious work, I need my steel-toed work boots. After years of hard labour they are looking a little worse for wear, but since they are as comfortable as slippers, I can't risk replacing them. It's strange but true: I can do heavy tasks with those boots on. Use the wood splitter, stack logs, run the tractor. Just give me the boots and proper work gloves and I'm happy to do stuff I'd never attempt in running shoes and garden gloves.

My hiking boots are only good for cold winter walks. They're supposed to be warm to some incredibly low temperature, but that's only if I keep moving! They are pseudo country fashion items, and besides, the soles can be slippery on icy patches. I solved that by getting those metal ice tracker affairs that slip over your boots. Not pretty, but practical, and that's what I need.

So every morning as I prepare for the outdoors, I check on the conditions, and reach for the proper boots. I hope it doesn't snow too soon, as I'm not sure how the famous rubber boots will be when it's really cold, but I think I'll buy some of those grey wool socks such as loggers wear and see if they will get me through the winter. If not, they will be waiting for spring, and once again I'll pull on the boots, a happy country camper.

So here's my wish for all of you: warm feet on cold nights. I'd add to that warm legs to tuck cold toes against. Just be prepared that you might be the one providing the legs!

Be prepared for a ride on my high horse. Sometimes I need to vent, and this is one of those! We never did find the culprit here, but at least I felt better when I'd let fly with what my father called our Irish temper!

THE GOOD, THE BAD, AND THE MALICIOUS

Give me a second to haul on my riding boots, and you might want to tighten the string on your hat there. We're saddling up the high horse, and you're going to have to hold on tight! We'll feed old Nellie while we see where we're riding.

It's no secret that I'm a big Hub booster. That little store does so much good for this community, and all on the generosity of donations. The highlight of the Hub Christmas party is returning that generosity. There were loud cheers as nearly $10,000 was pledged back to worthy causes benefiting everyone from youths to seniors. We're all very proud of that, and so should everyone be who contributes to or buys from our congenial store. That's the good part.

So climb onto that saddle now. We're off.

As the frosty nights set in before Christmas, the usual clutch of young people moved from the cold benches in the park to the warmth of the Hub lobby. No problem there - so far! However, as push led to shove, so to speak, someone crashed through the main door, leaving a pile of broken glass, two frightened women inside, and not a trace of the culprits. It took 18 women working three days to make up the amount needed to replace this door. AND this is the second time we have had to do it!! Of course, those responsible will not be apprehended. I ask you, why is the Hub a target for such shenanigans? We are the very people who support youth. We tolerate their insolent behaviour outside our store, we watch while they litter the pretty park across the street. but still we defend them as young people trying to find themselves.

111

From where does this disrespect for our town come? When the ice cream stand is attacked, when the antique shop and the candy shop have windows broken, when the liquor store is broken into, we have a major problem. We are all to the point of having to expend great quantities of time and resources repairing the vandals' damage and protecting ourselves against the bullying tactics of a few cowardly individuals who get some vacuous joy in the destruction of property. There are other individuals just as cowardly who know the perpetrators of these acts but won't divulge it. This whole process is a total waste of human endeavour.

And don't give me the old line that the young people have nothing to do. I'm not buying it! Look at all the wonderful accomplishments of the high school student council, how busy they have been, and what positive results have followed. Look at the group who mounted the puppet shows that they performed at schools and for the community. Young people who have taken it upon themselves to make a difference by being pro-active are an asset the indolent should aspire to emulate. It happens too often that we are slapped with the acts of the few who unfortunately tarnish the significant contributions of the many.

Somewhere the concept of respect has been lost. Children learn at an early age how far they can push parental patience, and a parent who will try to reason with a two-year old is letting that little one take the reins of power. Respect goes right off the track. In no time, the parent is the victim of a sassy youngster who knows there will be no retaliation. School days bring little change. Children stampede down the halls with no regard for anyone but themselves. They stand on sidewalks blocking traffic, throwing their trash wherever they like, and defying school authorities to correct the situation. Oh, they know their rights! They can smoke not three feet from the front door of the school, since they are on public property. Adult hands are tied, no one can react, and we all have to tolerate the mess left in the wake of this total disregard for the areas we share.

Respect is another word for simple manners, which seem to be in short supply these days. There is frequently a gaggle of young people congregated near the front of the Hub, but they will watch in total indifference as a person struggles in with numerous bags and boxes. Is this how they act at home or at school? Likely! We shouldn't have to ask for common courtesy. Somewhere along the line they have missed that lesson, though, so to avoid further confrontation we allow them to get away with it.

The whole attitude expands when no correction is provided, and rudeness becomes the new norm. There is an attitude of self-importance that invades every aspect of life, from rude behaviour on the highways to the pervasive use of cell phones. Those of us old enough to know better are stymied in our efforts to avoid confrontations when epithets are let loose at the least provocation.

There is disregard for the law, disrespect for the peacekeepers in our community, and derision of our court system, which is often too slack when dealing with misdemeanors. I don't want people clapped into jails; I do want them to take responsibility for their actions, and stop this cycle of wanton destruction and damage control. I want parents to stop mollycoddling children and start laying down the ground rules early. I want teachers to have the authority to do their job without having to be all things to all people. Kids are in school to learn; make them responsible for their own success too. And I want kids to realize that the whole community is working very hard to ensure they can grow up in a safe environment with plenty of recreational facilities to entertain them. However, I also want them to be part of the solution, I want them to stand up to the challenge of being worthy participants in making our town a place of pride. It's not impossible; look to the teen youth group, Taking Young People Seriously, TYPS, for a perfect example of young people working hard and achieving much.

Nothing would make us happier than to have the person who went flying through our Hub door fess up to the deed, and help us repair the damage. Who knows, it could be the beginning of a great relationship for both of us. All it takes is a little courage, and I can assure you, that individual would have our fully supported respect..

Now, climb down. Nellie's had enough for today. Back to the barn with you, old girl!

I'm nutty about getting the Christmas lights up. I love to see the sparkles reflecting through the trees and glistening with new snow. But oh my, it can be a trial.

LET THERE BE LIGHTS!

Can you see it? Can you hear it? Could you possibly miss it even if you tried?? It's the Christmas hype as palpable as plum pudding gushing from every media source imaginable. On November 1, the Christmas elves move in and overnight we are inundated with bows and finery fit for a palace, while every hardware store worth its salt has an array of Christmas lights to send Edison into raptures!

The displays are designed to make us want it all: flashy netting for shrubs, lacy icicles, the LED lights and the sparklers, to say nothing of the ones that automatically play random carols. And then, there's the fancy new apparatus for attaching them to the house. Now, there would be a piece of equipment any husband would cherish! There's no denying that outdoor lighting is next to mandatory to stave off the dark December that is coming. I admit it: I buy into it every year, confident this will be the time we "do it right".

We vow every year to put up the lights on a nice day, no waiting around for December 10. Let's get them up when it's decent and only turn them on later. We vow to get them out of the basement in plenty of time to get replacement bulbs, in November, say. We vow to have them all ready with the proper extension cords just waiting for the best day. It never happens.

Some time in late November I discover the boxes of lights behind the furnace, and haul them out for the big test. Alan knows what's about to happen, and takes the dogs for a walk. So there I sit, in a sea of tangled wires - which I know I did not leave like that last January - screwing bulbs into tiny sockets, sorting bad from good, and

114

mangling any organized colour arrangement we had. I've got a million orange bulbs and only two white ones; now I've got red next to orange and green next to purple. And where did that flashing one come from? Three are broken in the sockets involving the use of pliers and band-aids. Oh my, I do enjoy this job.

Since the day is looking promising, I think we should get at the hanging job right after lunch. Even suggesting it makes the weather turn immediately ugly. But now I am committed, and the calendar is screaming DECEMBER, so there's nothing left but to have at it. I can't figure out why Alan isn't into the holiday mood here, but he deigns to get into the planning phase as if it were a trip to the paint store. "Just get the darn things up, and don't worry about the colour!" Now, I ask you, is that sporting? What would the neighbours think of a hodge-podge of lights festooned haphazardly across the front of the house?

No, out comes the ladder, and he does his duty, hooking every light on those miserable little plastic clips that destroy fingernails and temper at an alarming rate. It takes us only two hours with frozen fingers and a dog dangerously close to the live wires to conquer the front eaves. Ah, the beauty!

We're one third done, and the novelty is beginning to wear thin. Alan suggests a coffee break to regroup, but I just know that if we stop we will be left with a half-decorated house, so we soldier on. Up and down the ladder he trundles while I feed out the lines of lights, reworking the colour scheme to no avail. We aren't talking much by now, as the lightness of the mood is dulled by the pain in our cold toes.

At last we reach the trees. Now, this should be the crowning glory of our work, since this is the side of the yard visible all the way up our road. We had notions of stringing the lights high in the oak tree, and bought a long pole whereby we could get them up about twelve feet in an orderly fashion, but I think the pole got used for a garden stake because it's nowhere to be found when we need it. Instead we resort to the very professional method we have seen the NCC workers using: throwing the strings of lights as high as we can, like a basket-ball player aiming for a 20-foot hoop. We swing them through the ironwoods, twist them around the spruce trees, and about twenty minutes after dark, consider that the whole miserable job is done. We've used enough extension cord to fence a coral; there are about fourteen strings of lights out there, and let me tell you, when we throw the switch for all those babies, we have light!

We also have chilblains, frozen fingers, sore feet, and a real need for a glass of spirits. It takes very little to convince us we have once again done a super job of decorating for Christmas, and anyway when the night is dark and the snow is falling, the whole thing will be a scene right out of the House Beautiful magazine.

When we drive by a house with Christmas lights still up in July, Alan is sure there is a husband laughing at the rest of us scrambling around in the cold of December and the snow of January wrestling with pesky decorations while he sits snug in the knowledge his decorating is done permanently! It won't happen that way at our house, but when it's -10, it sure looks tempting!

I wish you all a Christmas lit with lights on the outside and with love on the inside. And just a small dish of that rich plum pudding!

Here's a recipe you can quite literally take to the bank! I'll bet you a loonie you'lll want to make it.

THE RECIPE FOR A TRADITION

As reliable as the Eaton's catalogue, Grandma came for Christmas. She travelled by Greyhound, and December first we'd gather her up, her bulky old leather suitcase, her own pillow, and always the cardboard box. "Now leave that alone. It's presents." Her arrival signaled the start of the holiday for our family. We'd crowd into the house, settle Grandma in the guest room, and have "tea". Well, we children had tea; Grandma had a "teensy glass of sherry, dear." When she felt rested, she'd ceremoniously open the box to give us "the December present". This was the best! It was something we could enjoy while waiting for the magical 25th, a snowball ornament, a music box, maybe even a box of chocolates, one for each day.

There was one December present we will never forget. Grandma had made a brilliant wall hanging, a marvellous patchwork Christmas tree, obviously a year's work, all appliquéd, quilted in gold thread and decorated. There were twenty-three little scrolls of wrapping paper tied on like ornaments, each big enough to hold a trinket, and around the edge, Grandma had quilted "Loving and Giving make Happy Living." We were amazed by her careful stitching, and excited to think what treasures were hidden in all those wee packets. The wall hanging got a place of honour in the dining room, where everyone could admire the intricacies of her beautiful work.

"Now, children," Grandma said, "I know you've got a list longer than my arm, so many things you want. But this Christmas I'm giving you a gift that is going to last forever. I'm letting you share yourself, which is going to leave you feeling so good about yourself. Just for a little while, I want you to give some thought to those around you." It was a novel approach to Christmas, but Grandma had a way of reaching our hearts.

117

December 1, we reached into a little pocket in the trunk section of our patches tree, and drew out a gold fabric bag. Inside in Grandma's writing was this letter.

"My Dear Ones,

I'm giving you a Christmas challenge. Every day you can open one scroll ornament and you will find a note. Do as I ask, and soon you will know the true spirit of Christmas. Love, G."

Hmmm, an empty bag wasn't much to get!

Day Two, the little scroll contained a note that read, "Into the gold bag, place one penny for every fork in your house." We had thirty-eight forks!

Day Three: "Sit down beside me. Two cents for every chair, please."

Day Four: "Come to table means good food. Three cents for every table."

Day Five. "Did you sleep well? Five cents for each bed."

Day Six. "Are you seeing the light? Four cents for every lamp in the house."

Day Seven. "Six cents for every pair of mitts that warm your hands."

Day Eight "Five cents for every tap in the house. Cleanliness is a privilege."

Day Nine. "Be thankful for friends. Five cents for each telephone."

Day Ten. "Eight cents for your library card. Reading is a joy."

Day Eleven. "Are your feet warm? Two cents for each pair of shoes."

Day Twelve. "Listen to the world, ten cents for each TV and radio, please."

The bag was bulging! But we were all into Grandma' s challenge and recognizing our good fortune with every day. So on we went: twelve cents for each large appliance, eight cents for each newspaper, five cents for each toothbrush, twenty-five cents for our vehicles, three cents for each can in the cupboard, two cents for each light on our Christmas tree, two cents for every card we received, two cents for each item on our Wish List, five cents for each bike, skate, pair of skis, etc., four cents for each box of breakfast cereal in the cupboard.

On December 23rd, the little note read, "Now, aren't you the most fortunate family to have so much to be thankful for? You can spill out the bag and count your blessings. With joy in your heart, I want you to take what you have accumulated to a charity that needs it. Count your blessings, as you have one for each of the pennies you've accumulated. The best we have we give away to increase its value a hundredfold. I love you all. G."

We did as she had asked and were amazed at our collection. And indeed we gave the money to a local service club to which my dad belonged. It could have bought food for the Food Bank, toys for the Angel Tree, clothes for a new baby, pet food for the animal shelter, wood for a family's winter, a warm coat for a single mom, treats for seniors, and on the list goes. You can imagine how amazed two little girls were to discover many had less, far less, than they did. A lesson like this one is priceless!

We were awash in good spirits when we delivered our Christmas gold bag.

There was one more little pocket to open. For the 24th, Grandma wrote, "A penny for your thoughts. Use nice paper and your best writing to write a note to someone who has changed your life this year, someone you really appreciate and perhaps didn't tell. Let them know how much they mean to you. This is an angel letter."

I could tell you now that Christmas morning we held hands and sang, like in "The Grinch...", but no, we all had presents, we all had too much to eat, and we all gloried in the usual Christmas fare. However, we also harboured a wonderful glow brought about by Grandma's Patches Tree.

Now, if you want to share in that grand spirit of loving and giving, make yourself a Patches Tree. In fact, make several, it's a message that could change the world a penny at a time!

If I'd called this a project, you'd have run a mile, we all have such busy lives around Christmas. Start this in November to really enjoy it. You'll be glad you did!

THE PATCHES TREE - A STARTING POINT

What I'm giving you is the basic pattern. I know you're going to embellish it with a personal touch. The project is geared to beginner sewing level, so you and your family can all share in the creation. After all, you are making an heirloom here.

Read this all the way through to get a feel for it before you start.

You will need:

1. Scraps of fabric of at least three colours. If buying new fabric, 10 centimetres each of three co-ordinating colours will be enough.
2. Cotton broadcloth, about 23"x27" in a plain colour as a background for your design. If buying new, you will need .75 metre.
3. Strips of contrasting cotton for a frame around the background. You can get an extra 20 centimetres of one of the patch fabrics, if you like.
4. Backing fabric, cotton or muslin, patterned or plain, about 28"x32"for the back side of the project. (You might have some old sheeting at home that you could use for this, since it won't be seen when the hanging is on the wall.)
5. Quilt batting, 28"x32".
6. Various trims, ribbons for tying on the little scrolls, (narrow ribbon about 6 metres if you are buying new), tiny ornaments, stars, sequins, etc., to decorate your tree. Here's where your imagination can run rampant!
7. A length of dowel or a nice branch about three feet long and a length of ribbon to hang your tree on the wall.

Assembly:

1. Cut a triangle pattern from sandpaper or stiff cardboard, making it 3" across the base, and 3" high in the centre. Join the points to make a triangle. **Be sure to add ¼"on all sides for your seam allowance!!**

2. From your various colours, cut 36 triangles. Hint: stack the fabrics and cut several at once. Use a rotary cutter and a ruler for really accurate lines. It's important the triangles are all the same, or you'll never get the seams to line up, and your tree will be a Charlie Brown special!

3. Have a look at the diagram. Start assembling your tree by laying out 11 triangles, the first on its base, the next on its point, side by side to make your first row.

4. Your next row will have 9, set in the same manner.

5. Your next row has 7, with the following row having 5, the next 3, and the top a single triangle sitting on its base.

6. Fiddle with the design until you like the pattern and then, starting at the bottom row, using ¼" seam allowance, sew each line of triangles into a strip. Try to use an exact seam allowance so your triangles will go together neatly. Press all seams to one side, not open.

7. Sew the strips to each other until you have one big triangle. That's your "tree." Cut a small square about 3½"x2" and add it to the centre of the bottom row. That's the tree trunk. (It could be made like the little pocket for the original letter if you want.)

8. This next step takes a bit of patience. Press your tree very carefully, since the outside edges are bias and will stretch. Turn under ¼" on all raw edges. I used fabric glue to hold them in place - pins just wouldn't keep it straight! Now, place the tree in the centre of your background piece (#2 above), and stitch all around the edges of your tree. The machine zig-zag stitch works well, but hand sewing is the best. Press it after you've got it sewn in place.

9. Add strips of fabric (#3 above) cut 2½" wide to each side of the background piece to make a frame. You can get fancy here, and make a ruffle or piece the frame, or just go plain.

10. On the top edge of the frame add hanging strips. Cut 4 pieces of fabric 4½"x2½." Fold each piece lengthwise with right sides together, and sew a ¼" seam on the long edge. Turn right side out and press. Fold each piece in half, and stitch to the top edge of the frame evenly spaced with raw edges together. (The loops will be hanging upside down on the front of your design at this point.)

11. Lay your design face UP on a flat surface. Lay your backing piece (#4 above) face DOWN on top of your design. Line up the edges. Lay the quilt batt on top of the backing piece. Smooth everything and match all the edges. You may need to trim edges so they are all even. That's all right; this isn't going to be marked by your Home Economics teacher. Now, pin around all four sides. Sew around all four sides, using a ¼" seam allowance and making sure you are catching all layers, and leaving an opening at the bottom, about 6" long. This is going to take a while, sorry!

12. Turn the whole thing right side out, and press the edges lightly. Sew up the bottom seam by hand. Voila! There it is! Now quilt wherever you like, along the edges, around the tree, just go for it.

13. Attach the centre of ribbons about 10" long at each point of the triangles to tie on your scrolls. You will need 24. Stitch right through the backing to stabilize the batt and add "puff" to your design.

14. Using wrapping paper with a white backing, cut out 24 3"x3" squares for the little scrolls.The message can be written on the plain side, so when they are rolled they are like little decorations. Tie them onto the tree with the ribbons.

15. You'll need a dowel or nice branch to stick through the loops at the top, and you can attach the ends of a fancy ribbon to either end of the dowel or branch to hang your Patches Tree.

Make a ceremony of hanging the tree on the last day of November, and every day open one scroll. You can save the pennies in a jar or make the fancy little bag like Grandma did.

Wouldn't it be a Christmas miracle if this project appeared in every home over the holidays? Couldn't we make a difference, one penny at a time?

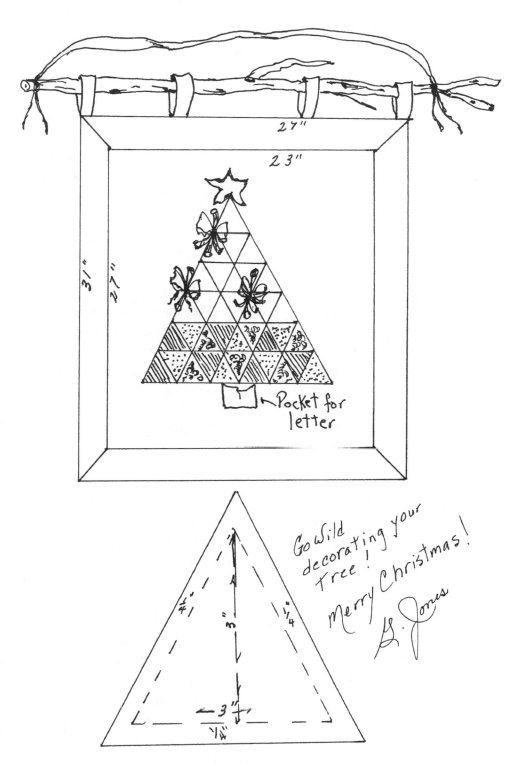

27"

23"

31"

27"

Pocket for letter

Go Wild decorating your Tree!

Merry Christmas!

G. Jones

4"

3"

1¼"

3"

¼"

¼"

"DEAR DIARY..."

I have a friend who has kept a faithful record of her life from the time she could pick up a pencil, age 6, I think. Every major event has been recorded for posterity. The daily living is documented too: the weather and the shopping trips. She has volumes stored in boxes, and even if she never reads them, at some point a grandchild might open that box, and see his grandmother come alive in her own handwriting.

In this day of computers we spurn concrete records such as bulky diaries or photo albums. In the future there is going to be precious little over which to reminisce. Our son came within a hair's breadth of losing every one of his family photos when his computer was left on an airplane. Imagine his relief in recovering that!

"June 2, 1994...Yes! Footings for the house were poured today. Neighbours dropped over to watch..."

I never thought I'd have the perseverance to keep a diary. However, while we were in house building mode I kept a record of every day's activities. For six months, I recorded every detail of the process, including our woods walks, robin sightings, etc. Interesting to read back over the time, and remember the exciting discoveries we were making about living in the country.

The diary business went by the board as we settled into daily doings that didn't seem to have any importance - why would I need that information? Then in 1997 we were given the famous 10-year Lee Valley Garden Journal. What a challenge! We realized we had a formidable task to keep records for the full ten years. That book could keep us entertained for a long time, but truthfully I expected it would lie forgotten on a shelf before January was out.

"Jan. 1, 1997 …6 cm. Snow…put the decorations away and had a good ski…"

The pristine pages beckoned, and we began the journal with enthusiasm. (My mother's expression when asked what she planned to do any given day: "Pile up what I did yesterday.") We have shared the responsibility for entering the morning temperature, the weather, and the highlights of the previous day. Alan also filled in the details about our gardens: the layout of the vegetable beds, the purchase of new plants, etc. It's a thorough record of the evolution of our property over ten years. We have saved newspaper clippings on special days, and noted family birthdays, so that as we turn the pages year by year we can see them again.

"Oct. 21, 2003. Pouring rain, thunder and lightning. A to work, G. ironing, mending…"

The diary lives on our kitchen counter where we can refer to it often. When one of us says we can't remember such a wet October, we can turn back to ten years of Octobers to find this very same weather. How's October 21, 2003 for an exciting day?? There are many like that, full of mundane activities that mark the passage of time. But aren't we glad to have those? Of course, since what it means is that all is right with our world, no crisis in need of attention. Just sun or rain, leaves being raked, wood stacked, laundry dried.

"June 4, 2002…sunny at 6 a.m. Paris born at 2:28, got to hear her cry at 6:30. Rosebreasted grosbeaks on butternut tree, robin in spruce tree. Good day."

From time to time, the daily rhythm is interrupted with exciting news, like the birth of our grand daughter. We stack that June day beside others and they pale by comparison. One year on that day we picked wild strawberries, once planted tomatoes, once attended a play rehearsal, but no June 4 would ever be as exciting as that day in 2002.

"Jan. 6, 1998. .5 degrees C at 7:30. Power out at 5:30, heavy ice storm during night...trees broken...Sound of ice melting on trees is something else..."

A full record of our ice storm ordeal follows: the six days with no power, the busy time melting snow for water and the camaraderie of our neighbourhood dinner party. A couple of years later we were walking in the woods, seeing wild turkeys.

"Nov. 28, 2005. Freezing rain...started splitting wood at 10 - finished 4:30 - half done ...stiff, tired"

The interesting thing is that often when we peruse previous years, we can relive the experience exactly. The diary entry is only five lines, but sometimes the effort recorded tells a much bigger story. There's the painting episode, the rock work, the trail clearing. There are the play rehearsals, the big opening nights, the evening we entertained John Crosbie (too nervous to eat his dinner!) There are the joyous days we got our two dogs and our cat, the sad days we bade farewell to our previous cats, the day we picked blueberries while it thundered violently.

"Nov. 29, 2002. D. here to pull pump, wires broken, 3 hrs. in snowy weather to repair, Shawn here to fix cupboards...4 cm snow."

There's more stuff in this diary. We can go back and find all the house repairs; funny thing, I have neglected to put in what each one cost us. Is that selective memory? Just when we are thinking an item is "a year or two old," I find the entry that makes it nine years old. Time sure goes fast when you're having fun.

Every page in this wonderful diary will be filled on December 31, and we are angling for a new journal. How else will we be able to keep track of when we brought the fish in from the ponds, what the mileage is on the car, when we seeded the garden? How else will we be able to see the regular activities of our full and active life?

As the days wind into years, we are amazed to see how one February will be much like the rest. We see the rhythm and pattern of our lives as we read through the daily entries, truly a time for everything: a time to plant, a time to reap, a time to laugh and a time to cry. They're all there in our ten-year journal. Perhaps at some point our grand children will open this dog-eared book and discover how happy we have been here, Maybe too they will see the pleasure we have derived, not only from the large events that shape our lives, but also the daily details that define us. Then they will know that life's blessings come by enjoying every moment. Time is precious, spend it wisely.